MW01614436

What I

And His

FRESH Awareness Workshop

"The tools in the Fresh Awareness Workshop unlock doors that may have been previously shut to what is wanted and needed. They can help break through generational issues!" **- Kathy Malhotra, Grief Recovery Certified Consultant**

"I would say definitely take the Fresh Awareness Workshop because you will discover things about yourself that you can't find anywhere else. Before this class I was skeptical but now I support it 100%" **- Cameron Quiseng**

"The Fresh Awareness workshop is excellent for my life before this class I used to harbor all sorts of anger and fear and I would end up taking it out on my girlfriend and family. I realize why I do the things I do and now I am confident that I can change my future and help others more as result." **- Donny Briske**

"The Fresh Awareness workshop helped me to understand why I was getting stuck and has given me the tools to break free of my repeating cycles so that I can truly become the woman God created me to be." **- Teana Henderson**

"Make time! The Fresh Awareness Workshop empowers you and helps you specifically identify where the voices of doubts come from and how to specifically conquer them." **- Derrex Brady**

"I highly recommend taking the Fresh Awareness workshop! To be aware of yourself, is the only way to change. Find out who you are and why you do what you do; give yourself freedom." **- Marina Quinonez**

"Before I came to the Fresh Awareness Workshop I was not so sure how helpful it would be but because I am open to self improvement I decided to come and very HAPPY to have done so. I now have the tools to attack the enemy in my mind and Dream the way that God wants me to!" **- Angelica Mariscal**

"I came not really knowing what to expect. The Fresh Awareness Workshop helped me to recognize things that were happening in my life that I hadn't realized. Now I feel that I have the tools necessary to make a change in myself and to connect better with people around me. I now have a strong base to begin a path to a great relationship with my son." **- Jose Castro**

"I highly recommend the Fresh Awareness workshop. The tools provided bring you straight to the root of the very things that stop you from moving ahead and fulfilled your dreams. It's a safe environment that practically takes you through a process of breaking through. It's so powerful. Do this now and change your circumstances!" **- Vicki Hagadorn, Grief Recovery Certified Specialist**

"This is worth it-without a doubt! Find a way to get yourself there. My husband and I began using the tools on the first day and were able to do away with a recurring pattern that has blocked me in our marriage for the past 2 years! I am so grateful and eager to keep applying what I've learned." - **Chinue Black**

"This was so earth shattering for me. Suddenly I could see that the "fog" and cycle of impotence, depression, sadness, futility and fear was not a fog at all, but part of my defense mechanism working very wisely on so many areas of my heart. I became shrewd. I was awakened. Re-inspired me to trust whole heartily and to Dream! It gave me back permission to Dream!" - **Kamilah Dozier**

"Helped me to identify automatic and unconscious responses in my life. For the first time the dreamer in me had an uninterrupted platform to speak clearly and confidently, without fear of being cut-off or shut down. I no longer have to be a prisoner of my past and allow it to unconsciously control me." - **Tony Brewer**

" It made me see how much hope I've lost. I haven't been dreaming for a long time. This seminar gave me hope to dream again. It allowed me to dig deep and not be afraid to be open. It helped me connect with my emotions." - **Lynn Brewer**

"The FRESH awareness workshop was an amazing experience for me. Before the seminar, I was clouded with a lot of insecurity and just a general sense that I was worthless or powerless to change. After some very moving moments in the seminar, in which the fellow participants really spoke truth to my heart after the teaching helped my heart to receive it, I felt so free! It was like I knew myself again, my true self, and nobody's reactions or rejection could keep me from being okay with being me. I really understood and BELIEVED that I am lovable and valuable, just as I am." - **Shaela Druyon**

"Before taking the Fresh Awareness Workshop I had damaging behaviors that were showing up in my relationships, particularly my marriage. As much as I wanted to be different, I could not seem to break through. I was even more frustrated, because I have done many workshop and other types of therapies. The Fresh awareness Workshops not only showed me what was causing my behaviors it gave me the tools to be different. This workshop helped save my marriage. I would highly recommend this to anyone who is seeking more and knows they have more to offer as a person." - **Sandi Atmore Grief Recovery Certified Specialist**

"Before the Fresh Awareness Workshop I was unable to identify what was keeping me from breaking free from habits I've had for many years, "bad" habits. This workshop showed me how to slow down my thought process, to interrupt the habit while it's happening. Identify why I'm doing what I do and how to change it. It's AMAZING....REALLY!" - **Michael K. Jackson**

FRESH Awareness:
The Battle Within

By Mikki Wade

FRESH Awareness: The Battle Within

Copyright © 2012 by Mikki Wade

ISBN 978-0-615-74334-9

Printed in the United States of America

Dedication

To Tony Brewer: a best friend, mentor, and spiritual warrior. I always told you that you had a book inside of you. I believe this is that book. You have inspired me and given me the courage to finish this book. I know you're laughing from above. I miss you and love you very much.

Table of Contents

Chapter 3: Financial Awareness 59

Chapter 4: Health Awareness 101

Chapter 5: Spiritual Awareness 125

Conclusion: The Architect of You 165

About The Author 167

ACKNOWLEDGMENTS

This book took me about 8 years to write. Within these years there have been several influential people who directed me on my path to finish this book. This book could have not been written without the help and support I received from them.

First I would like to thank God, who is the reason I started writing and inspired me to believe that this message should be in the hands of many people.

I am forever thankful for Garrett Duenes who help edited in the very first draft of this book. He has inspired me to be who I am today. He believed in me when I didn't believe in myself.

I'm indebted to James Bean who helped review and edit my book over several years. His honest feedback allowed me to push me to improve myself and increase my knowledge what I wrote.

I also owe a debt of gratitude to John Steinreich who not only inspired me by his example of writing and self publishing his book but also gave his time and effort to edit parts of this book.

For Kamilah Dozier who also helped to edit and make sense of what I wrote in the earlier stage of the book. She inspired me by giving me great feed back after reading the book.

I would also like to thank Ade Agbalaya, Eric Hall, Derrick and Susan Williams, Chantel Steinreich, Lynn Brewer, Kris Kovacs, Amy Frost and all of my spiritual family in the Turning Point Church. You have inspired me by your trust and love.

To all the people who attended my Fresh Awareness Workshops and those who took Grief Recovery with me: Thank you for your support and trusting me with your hearts. Your heart to seek healing has inspired me to put this book out there for you.

I owe an enormous amount of gratitude to Nilsa Manibusan, who took an 8 year unending project and finished editing this book in 8 months. I truly could not have finished this book without her feedback and the wisdom she added to this book. There are not many people you find that can read your mind. Nilsa has that ability to understand what I was thinking and make sense for the readers. Her patience, and all the time she put into this book went beyond the call of duty. This book is as much hers as mine, and I am thankful I had a chance to work with someone who not only reads but applies what she reads. She is an amazingly talented professional editor.

To Tony Brewer, a best friend and someone who will forever inspire me to go after my dreams: I dedicate this book to him. Even though He is no longer walking on this earth with me He has been a motivating force behind this book. He was and still is my spiritual armor bearer. He was, and is, not only closer than a brother, but he fathered my heart into a spiritual man. He pushed me to be the best me I can be.

Finally, my deepest thanks go to my family. To my mother Stephanie Wade, whose love I will forever cherish in my heart. I know she was watching over me as I wrote each word. My Father, who by moving to Africa, inspired me by his example to risk everything and go after my dreams. My personal stories that I shared this book were a major risk for me, but his example allowed me to take that risk.

My daughter Sophie who started writing her books at the very early age of 6 years old also inspired me to finish what I started. Her natural writing talents and love for writing has inspired me to persevere throughout this journey. Similarly, I'm thankful to my son, Mikki Wade, for his example from the age of 3 until now for persevering in his acting career and not giving up after going from audition to audition. He taught me to not quit even when I don't see the light at the end of the tunnel.

My niece Megan who is like a daughter to me, her leadership qualities and drive to be the best has help embraced my leadership as an author. I'm also grateful for my sister Karen Wade, who consistently gave me time to write by taking care of my children while I was engaged in writing this book. She also spoke life into me as she encouraged me by acknowledging how proud she is of me.

Last but not least, my deepest thanks to my wife without whom I would have given up writing a long time ago. She believed in me at every stage of this book from the first page until the last. Throughout all the years we have been married she has been my biggest fan. Her support and love gave birth to this book.

Introduction

Is life supposed to be passing you by and you have no control over the outcome? Is life supposed to be about getting up and rushing out the door in such a routine that you feel like you are sleepwalking through life? What if you could predict your future? What if your life was not a random series of lucky and not so lucky moments? What if you could understand yourself more that you ever have?

I wanted desperately to find out the answers to these questions. My life was passing me by as if I was watching a movie. It felt like the minute I woke up someone else took over my body and went about living my life for me and I would get my body back as I was about to fall asleep at the end of the day. I was not living. I was operating like a machine.

I got extremely frustrated with my life feeling like it was a rerun of an old movie. I knew the lines, what the next scenes would look like, and how the movie would end. I wanted to go through my days so fast in order to get to the next day, because I couldn't stand watching my life go by. I'm sure I'm not the only one who goes through this cycle. We all have become busier, unconsciously living, and unaware of the results we are producing. Our attention is constantly pulled by our next appointment, or the next new book, ideas or trend. All these "new" things only excite us for a short while until we need to replace it with something more exciting.

Life seems more and more to be without a purpose. Divorce is on the rise and so is our emotional stress. Our health is on the decline even though we claim to live longer. Our spiritual life seems to be slipping away as we rush through our days. We are eating but not really enjoying the food. We are too busy living and yet not able to really enjoy life. Our lives are supposed to be easier and more connected through text, email, Facebook, Twitter, Skype, cell phones, voice mails, videos, etc., but we can still be disconnected emotionally and feel alone. How did we get here?

I woke up one day and decided to pursue the answers to these questions above. I was sick and tired of being sick and tired. I knew I couldn't blame my lack of connection to life on the people who designed these things that are supposed to make my life convenient. I chose to live this way: maybe not consciously, but subconsciously. My journey led me to study and live out the scriptures, attend several seminars, read countless books, get personal coaching, and I spent close to six figures in the process. I wanted to know why and how I kept getting unwanted results in my life. Even though I had seen these patterns in my life in just about everyone I knew, I realized that these came from an internal system which can be turned on or off.

I eventually found the answers I was looking for and now I would like to share them with you in this book. Life is not meant to be lived like the movie *Groundhog Day*. It's not meant to feel like a rerun of a movie. I invite you to take a journey with me to discover the root of the problems in your life. I will share my struggles and beliefs with you and how I overcame them. I focus on five main areas in life; Finances, Relationships, Emotions, Spirituality and Health. These spell out F.R.E.S.H. These main areas have sets of patterns that are easily predictable, yet most people don't realize what they are or where they come from. If these patterns are left unchecked they can completely rob you from living a life that you were designed to live. We will dig in to the root of the patterns and learn how to change these patterns. You will gain a F.R.E.S.H. Awareness of your life.

I believe the most frustrating thing in life is not knowing "why" life is turning out to be the opposite of what we had hoped for. There is battle within you constantly raging over your mind, heart and soul. This book will take you on a journey that will challenge your perspective of your life. You will be able to understand why you keep hitting a wall and haven't been able to break through it. You will learn tools to help you not only break through this wall, but stay on the other side. Life is too short to go to the grave not really fully living out your true potential.

Let's turn the page to the first step of your journey!

Chapter 1

EMOTIONAL AWARENESS

Pay Attention to the Warning Lights!

My first car was a 1982 blue Ford Mustang and I was extremely happy to have a car as a teenager. I also felt confident, having been given the responsibility to be trusted with a car. I remember studying for days for the driving test. After passing the written test, came the driving test. Even though I failed the first time by running a red light, it didn't stop me from coming back to pass the driving test. I finally got my license!

I will never forget the night I saw smoke coming out of my hood; the death of my car. I never really paid much attention to the warning light on my dashboard. I always told myself I would take care of it after I ran around picking up my friends and doing what some teenagers do to show off. That night, I was on my way home from my friends' house and I was flying on the freeway when the light on my dashboard kept flashing (as it had been for the past week), but this time the temperature gauge was very high. The car started smoking. It got my attention, so I pulled off the freeway. Having no knowledge of what I was doing (and not sure what to expect), I remember grabbing a rag to protect my hands, opening the radiator cap, and was shocked as an eruption of hot steam blew up into the air! I ran for cover so fast because I thought the whole car was about to blow up!

I never forgot that lesson. Most of all, I will never forget the next thing I did right after I almost burned myself; I filled up a container of cold water and poured it into the steaming radiator. For those of you who don't know much about cars, cold water over a hot engine can crack the engine. It did just that. I got back in my car and drove home, but white smoke came out the exhaust pipe and began to sputter: the death sign. The next day a mechanic told me I had definitely cracked my engine. My heart cracked as he told me the news. The cost to fix it was more than the value of the car itself.

I believe we all possess a dashboard which lets us know our emotional well-being. Our emotions act as indicators (just like the flashing light on my dashboard) to let us know there is something wrong. However, many of us don't pay much attention to that warning light, and when this light starts to bother us we tend to use the wrong information to handle the problem just like I did with my car by pouring cold water on a hot engine. The warning signs are not just for bad feelings but they are also for good feelings. If we don't pay attention to this warning, it will get worse just as it did when I didn't pay attention the maintenance light in my car by looking into the cause of the warning. Some of us need a quick oil change and some need a major tune up. Unless we address what is going on under the hood of our emotions, we run the risk of cracking the engine of our hearts and losing what we value the most.

The Birth of Emotional Patterns

"Our emotions are not dumb even when they do not make any sense. When we respect them we can start to understand them." ~ Mikki Wade

The things we believe about our emotions have a direct impact on how we deal with them. We all learn our behaviors and values from someone else. There was interesting research done by Dr. Morris Massey which gives us a big clue to where it all started:

Dr. Morris Massey has described three major periods during which values are developed.

1. *The Imprint Period.* Up to the age of 7, we are like sponges, absorbing everything around us and accepting much of it as true, especially when it comes from our parents. The confusion and blind belief of this period can also lead to the early formation of trauma and other deep problems. The critical thing here is to learn a sense of right and wrong, good and bad. This is a human construction which we nevertheless often assume would exist even if we were not here (which is an indication of how deeply imprinted it has become).

2. *The Modeling Period.* Between the ages of 8 and 13, we copy people, often our parents, but also other people. Rather than blind acceptance, we are trying on things

like suit of clothes, to see how they feel. We may be much impressed with religion or our teachers. You may remember being particularly influenced by junior school teachers who seemed so knowledgeable — maybe even more so than your parents.

3. *The Socialization Period.* Between 13 and 21, we are very largely influenced by our peers. As we develop as individuals and look for ways to get away from the earlier programming, we naturally turn to people who seem more like us. Other influences at these ages include the media, especially those parts which seem to resonate with the values of our peer groups. (Adapted from Wikipedia)

According to Dr. Morris' research, The Imprint Period (from birth to age 7 years), has a major impact on how we deal with and value our emotions. This is the age that I was told to keep my mouth shut even though I was hurting. Unfortunately, the examples most of us have had on how to deal with our emotions have not been very healthy. The information we learn from these examples becomes the blueprint we rely on when dealing with our emotions. My experience left me feeling that my emotions don't matter and are not valuable.

Growing up, I never saw my family cry much, but I remember hearing a lot of yelling. I never heard "I love you". When I cried I was told to stop either verbally or nonverbally. I vividly remember my mother abusing alcohol to numb her pain. What I learned from her example was to not deal with the pain, but to "numb out" by drinking away my problems. This all happened during my Modeling Period (from age 8-13 years) when I started to subconsciously copy my parents' behavior when dealing with pain. It also happened to be the time when I was intrigued by my mother's prayer and journaling habits which later influenced my decision about religion. (I will speak more about that in the chapter on Spiritual Awareness.)

I am not blaming my parents and this is not only about them. They followed a pattern from their parents and I would also guess that their parents did the same. The purpose of me sharing about my childhood is not for you to feel sorry for me, but for you to hopefully relate to where I learned the patterns on how to deal with my emotions.

Interestingly enough, as Dr. Massey concluded in his research, between the ages of 13 to 21 years (the Socialization Period) I naturally turned to other kids who were like me. I was subconsciously looking for validation from others who could relate to my pain. I was also attracted to any media that validated my pain. This was a part of my "numbing out" process I had learned as a young child. Society reinforced what I believed about emotions not being important. Phrases like "boys don't cry", or "cry baby" are some of the things I believe many of us heard growing up. Many times I didn't understand my emotions, and when I thought I did they were often illogical. My conclusion as a child was that my emotions are dumb and not valid. It led me to feel very insecure as a child. I was hoping that when I grew up I wouldn't feel all these emotions anymore. Yet, as an adult, whenever I felt something I would try to disregard my emotions or beat myself up for not having better control over them. In addition, I would act as if I didn't feel anything at all. I locked my emotions in a room of my heart and would leave them for dead. This was a losing battle. Even though I believed that my emotions were not important or a top priority they always seemed to find a way to interfere or influence every decision I made.

DEAD MAN Walking

When one buries their emotions they are in fact having a burial just as they would for a dead person. The dictionary defines burial as the act of putting a dead body in the ground. This would make sense if your emotions were dead (which we wish some of them would be), but your emotions are alive and valid. Imagine being buried alive. What would you do? You would probably kick and scream hoping someone would hear that you are still alive. Your goal would be to get out of that grave as fast as you can. Your emotions want the same thing: to be acknowledged, validated and released. When they finally do get out what happens? An eruption much like the steam erupting from the radiator of my car is typically the end result! This is when you have a fit of rage, you lose control, and everything seems to come out. The dead man comes out of the grave.

"The walls we build around us to keep sadness out also keeps out the joy." ~ Jim Rohn

Another thing that happens when we do not express our emotions is that we lose the joy of life. We stop enjoying life and we forget our heart's desires. We don't even know what we want anymore or what we feel. We get up go to work, come home and start dreading the next day. I remember hoping the days would end so I could get them over with. We are indeed living as a dead men and women walking. This is what happens when we bury the very thing which was meant to keep us connected to our hearts.

The reason we don't like to deal with our emotions is that we are afraid of what we will find when we allow ourselves to feel them. Dealing with many different people in my workshops it seems that a block always comes up when it comes to expressing emotions. It's usually connected to not having a voice growing up. As I shared with you, not being able to express how I felt when I was growing up did in fact take away the voice my emotions had. Another reason why we don't like dealing with our emotions is because we fear it may reveal the dark side of our emotions. No one likes to see that side of them. Therefore, we activate our defensive mechanism as a shield to protect ourselves from the danger of discovering our dark side.

Defense Mechanism

Sigmund Freud in his psychoanalytic theory said, "A defense mechanism is a tactic developed by the ego to protect against anxiety. Defense mechanisms are thought to safeguard the mind against feelings and thoughts that are too difficult for the conscious mind to cope with. In some instances, defense mechanisms are thought to keep inappropriate or unwanted thoughts and impulses from entering the conscious mind."

When you are not willing to deal with your emotions, past or present, you automatically activate a defensive mechanism to protect yourself from the truth. This mechanism causes you to choose to forget the pain in order to avoid some of your responsibilities by justifying, living in denial, projecting your pain on others, and ultimately rejecting the truth of how those buried emotions affect your daily life.

In order to bring more awareness to our defense mechanism, let us explore the behavior it causes us to have:

> 1. *Justification: To demonstrate or prove to be just, right, or valid. To declare free of blame; absolve. To free (a human) of the guilt and penalty attached to grievous sin.*[1]

> Justification always starts with the feeling that we are entitled to something. "I deserve this" is a phrase often used when we are justifying. Another way you can tell you're justifying is when you are trying to make yourself feel right about something you did or didn't do. Excuses are born with justification.

> 2. Denial: "*Denial stems from an internal preoccupation with avoiding pain. It is like a flashlight that works in reverse, casting shadows rather than light. It throws darkness over selected parts of the world to make them less noticeable, enabling us to hide embarrassing parts of our personality from our own vision; even though these parts may be obvious to everyone else...Denial prevents us from seeing things that make us too uncomfortable.*" ~Timmen Cermak

[1] *http://www.thefreedictionary.com/justified*

This happens when we don't believe in reality anymore. We don't want to face the pain attached to the emotions that come from facing the reality of the undesired results of our lives. To deny our reality is to check out emotionally, numb the pain so we can misplace the emotions or feel different while the pain still lurks inside.

3. _Projecting:_ This is the communication of the pain you see in yourself being played out in the person in front of you. In other words, we get mad at seeing our negative reflection in other people's character and behaviors. I believe that the passion you have to see justice, correction or healing done in someone else's life is the same justice, correction and healing your heart is yearning for. That's why the best advice you give is the one you need to hear the most.

The major problem with projecting when you are not dealing with or healing your own pain is that you become self-righteous. Self-righteousness is when you are appalled that someone would behave in a certain way and in response you pull out the correction stick and the blaming wand forgetting that you actually do the very same thing.

4. _Rejection:_ This is another way the body and the mind deal with new

information. When you are used to believing your programming about your emotions, your mind also believes and protects that belief from any threats of change. This is called homeostasis. Homeostasis is the body's natural resistance to change. It keeps the body in a condition of equilibrium. With this amazing self-regulating system we could adapt to any outward conditions. When the body gets hot it sweats to maintain a balanced internal temperature to keep us alive.

The problem with homeostasis is that it resists any changes, good or bad, to the body's equilibrium. For example, when you go running and you haven't in a while you're sending a shock to your body and your body's homeostasis will reject that change thinking you're causing danger to it. It doesn't care if you need to work out because you're unhealthy. Change is change whether it's good or bad. The great thing about this is when you train your body to accept the new balance it will adapt to that new balance. So homeostasis can work for you or against you. I say all this to say that ANY new information about changing your old belief system for your emotional state naturally causes your mind to reject new information even if it will help you.

By now you may be asking for a solution to this mad cycle. If you are, congratulations! You are on your way to self-awareness. With any changes you ever want to make in your life, the first step is always awareness. In other words, you can't go from A to Z without first knowing where A is. A represents your current emotional position in life, and Z represents where you want to be. Knowing where A is on the map of your life in order to get to Z is what I want to address next.

Healthy Resurrection of Our Emotions

The first step to changing your emotional behavior begins with the awareness of the fact that there is a problem. So far, we have talked about the price of not dealing with your emotions and how you choose to react or respond to them. As I mentioned before, your mind and body have believed and agreed for a long time about the way you deal with your emotions. This is a built-in emotional homeostasis. Even though you have been operating with this defense mechanism for a long time, you always have the freedom to choose how to respond to your emotions. You are NEVER without choice.

The Battle of Wills

Will: the mental faculty by which one deliberately chooses or decides upon a course of action. A desire, purpose, or determination, especially of one in authority.[2]

A wild elephant has tremendous strength, yet when a metal chain is attached to its leg in order to tame it, it starts to adapt to this new limitation. The elephant starts to associate pain with the chain, and as a result, does not attempt to break free anymore. It forgets the mighty strength it possesses. The painful memory of trying to

[2] *http://www.thefreedictionary.com/will*

20

break free triggers the belief of defeat. This is the point when the trained elephant's chain is changed to a rope. The rope, unlike the metal chain, can be snapped in seconds by the elephant. Since the brain already chose to lose the fight, the battle is not even fought. The elephant's will is now broken.

There are many strong people out there who started off with great willpower, but because they have lost so many battles, they have given up fighting all together. Our belief system, in regards to our emotions, has to obey a certain authority figure just like the elephant was controlled by a trainer. Even though this authority figure is our own voice or our own will, it has a desire, purpose, or determination to produce a result in line with our false self.

Our false self is the part of us still trying to protect ourselves from being our true self and living up to our full potential. I call that false self the "Protector" because it attempts to protect us from any pain even if that pain will produce growth. This is especially true if the pain reminds us of a pain we experienced in our childhood. This part of us operates with the negative label we put on ourselves and works to keep the negative belief systems in place so no changes will take place. As the elephant settled for a limited and restricted life by protecting itself from the pain, we too limit our life when we listen to the beliefs of our past pain.

A part of our mind and heart doesn't feel threatened by the voice of the Protector because we recognize and trust that voice. It feels more comfortable and safe to be in a state of protection even though we may actually be dying.

In other words we subconsciously believe in the false promise of a safe life and we justify our unsafe behavior regardless of the evidence of the painful results we produce by obeying that voice.

Yet, there's another side of us I call the Dreamer. This part of us wants the exact opposite of what the Protector wants. This is the person we all aspire to be; our true selves. The Dreamer is the person inside of us who desires to be free to express themselves without fear of rejection or a negative outcome. This is the bold, fearless child we were before we got hurt and started to shrink back from diving into life. Before the elephant was captured, it was in a Dreamer stage of life running freely and living without limit or restriction. The Dreamer's desire, purpose, and determination are the same: Freedom for you to live without self-imposed limits or restrictions and to for you to make choices in line with your true self.

How Does the Battle Play Out?

Let's say your heart's desire and belief is that you are worthy of love and respect, and that you are capable of succeeding in life. This would be a self-talk springing from your Dreamer. The opposite of the Dreamer's voice are the lies from the Protector causing you to fear that people will disrespect you, that you will be a failure, and that you are unworthy of being loved.

When you take on any new challenge in your life, like a job or changing something in your character, you'll usually experience inner resistance; the war starts. For instance, you may have a fear of being disrespected and it may trigger you to be defensive. You may hear the Protector's voice whispering that people don't care about you and that they'll disrespect you. You may hear the protector's voice tell you that you're not worthy of respect. You may then be triggered to hurt or disrespect others before they hurt or disrespect you. The Protector may persuade you to hide or run away from new responsibility or positions in order to protect you from being vulnerable and disrespected. Unfortunately, whenever you step out on a ledge or take on a leadership position, you'll leave yourself vulnerable for someone to disrespect or judge you.

The completion of this book triggered these very fears in me. However, I chose not to listen to that voice because I knew it was the voice of the Protector. If you believe the voice of these negative emotions and don't learn to control them, they will keep you from growing and cause you to perform in line with your false self.

Translating the Background Noise

The voices in your head are barely noticeable at first, like elevator music or background music at a restaurant or party. Eventually, you become unconscious of the background noise because you may be focused on a conversation or anything else that catches your attention. The negative voices start out the same way. First, they sound distinguishable, and pretty soon they become indistinguishable and you'll forget they're even there. You subconsciously learn to live with them and make them part of your identity and your belief system. These negative voices don't only come from your head; the negative talk is all around you. You hear them on news, ads, posters, internet, radio, commercials, at your job, in the lyrics of the music you listen to, and from the people around you.

There is also another voice always present in the midst of the negative battle: the Dreamer's voice. The voice of the Dreamer is positive and may sound like a whisper or an unrecognizable voice. It is very uncomfortable to accept it as your own voice. We're so used to hearing the other negative voices in our head that we have subconsciously disregarded this voice.

Have you ever disregarded a compliment by saying something like "I'm not all that, if you only knew everything about me."? That voice is not from your true self. It's the voice of the impostor, the Protector trying to disguise its voice to match yours. Why? So you won't fight him or her anymore and eventually accept it as your only voice. Remember, the Protector's job is to hide your true self and pretend to be the real you.

When you consciously separate the voices in your head, you can start to differentiate them from one another. You can now consciously reject the label you used to identify yourself with. Next time someone gives you a compliment, tell you them "Thank you. I receive that", even if you have a hard time accepting it at first. Making this a habit drives it deep into your subconscious mind training it to accept positive reinforcement. This also silences the voice of the Protector trying to stop the incoming reinforcement to the Dreamer.

For example, one day while I was driving, I started to feel this intense depression taking over me. I start to feel angry, mad, and sad and upset at myself for no apparent reason. It came out of nowhere. The battle was fierce. At first I tried to disregard it, but it got so intense I had to literally pull over on the road and grab a note pad. I knew the advice that I would give to someone going through this self-imposed verbal abuse: get the negative talk out of your head and put them on paper. In other words, expose light on your dark thoughts and emotions.

I started writing like a mad man, and I sure felt like one. I wrote out all of the negative self-talk in my head. After that, I started to feel better. But I knew it was not over and that I needed to take one more step: to translate the lies with the truth. In order words I needed to feed the Dreamer. I looked over my list and it looked as if someone else (who hated my guts) was in my head attempting to tear me apart from the inside out. I wrote things like,

25

"you're a deadbeat dad", "you're worthless", "you won't amount to anything", "you can't get things right", "you are never going to change", and so on. I fought back by writing true affirmation statements about my character, which was the very opposite of my negative self-talk. In addition to doing this, I called a friend of mine to share what happened. I subconsciously wanted affirmation from someone other than myself. This battle was so intense that a part of me was still wondering if what I heard the Protector say was true. My friend couldn't believe these negative messages and reassured me that these thoughts were so far from the truth of who I am. That reassurance rebuilt and strengthened the voice of my Dreamer.

The process I just described is the process that we subconsciously go through on a daily basis. There is a saying which is very true, "Your head is like a bad neighborhood, you don't want to go in there by yourself." We all have certain bad neighborhoods in our heads, and most of us go in these dark alleys alone and get jumped and assaulted. The scary thing is that some of us are so used to those bad neighborhoods that we decide to make them our permanent home.

One of the things you can do to fight back is to have someone else translate what you're thinking about yourself so they can be help you navigate back to sanity or a better neighborhood. Another thing you can do is, when attacked, you stop and write out your thoughts on paper and ask yourself if this identity or label matches your true self. When you do this you will automatically become conscious of this vicious cycle.

Diving Into The Battle Together

The Protector within you has an agenda for your life. Bluntly put, he wants to "protect" the old you by keeping things as normal and comfortable as possible. In my FRESH Awareness workshops, we dive right into the battle together. We uncover both sides of you and we figure out what is your Protector's plan of attack on your Dreamer. I have seen people who have taken the workshop write down their Protector's plan of attack and several months later completely forget what they wrote and unconsciously give into to that plan. Why? They usually stop working on breaking their cycles. They become too busy to deal with their voices. They don't feed the Dreamer's voice enough and their Dreamer start to starve. They get used to the elevator music in the background again because their attention is now focusing on something else.

The Protector's identity and survival depends on you becoming unconscious about your triggers and cycles. The Protector's negative label for you grows stronger when you obey it. How? When you unconsciously allow your behavior to match your label, the negative label you give yourself must create an environment to feed and fit that label. For example, if you label yourself as "unworthy to be loved", you won't feel worthy of love, and will subconsciously look for situations and people to feed and affirm that label.

We also tap into the other part of you in the workshop, the true you; the Dreamer. The most amazing thing about this part of you is that he or she is stronger than the

Protector. The fact that you've read this far tells me that your Dreamer is fighting hard to come out and that he or she is growing stronger. Many people in my workshop have reconnected with their Dreamer and created amazing results. Just like the negative label we put on ourselves changes our behavior and looks for a match of environment to grow and feed itself, the Dreamer's label (i.e., "you are worthy to be loved") also creates a behavior and an environment for the Dreamer to grow and thrive.

One of the most common things I hear from people in my workshops is that they have a hard time believing what the Dreamer has to say about them. It sounds like a fantasy or impossible to accomplish. This perception is triggered by an emotion that is rooted in fear: fear of not being good enough or not having what it takes to accomplish their dreams or to become the person they want to be. As a result, their dreams stay trapped in their hearts. If you believe that your dreams are impossible to achieve, then you are listening to the wrong voice. You're probably subconsciously choosing to listen to the Protector who is attempting to keep you trapped in a limited unfulfilled life.

One of the Protector's most effective strategies is to make you believe in a false security while he kills you from the inside out. Your ability to succeed and break this cycle is limited by the Protector's label of you, which you unconsciously adopt. The Protector will tell you that you are safe living in a shell and that sticking your head out in the unknown is too dangerous. Yet the Protector fails to mention that there is a price that you'll pay for living in that shell of protection: this shell will become your limited world and self-made prison or grave.

Fighting the Wrong Battles

Most of the time we spend much of our energy, and time protecting ourselves. We are fighting to protect our shell when we should be fighting to risk breaking out of our shell or prison. Many people fight everyone and everything around them without questioning who the real enemy is. They justify, deny, project and reject the true reality around them. Don't get me wrong, there are external triggers. Some of them can be difficult people who have a special ability of getting under our skins. Yet, if you keep battling all these people and running from them without taking responsibility for your reactions, you will be left alone with no friends. As I mentioned earlier, nothing changes until we take responsibility for the reaction to our emotions and circumstances. The battle that you should focus on is your inner battle. This will help you overcome your outer battles.

Peace is all that we want in a war, even though the first yearning is to win. Many win the battles but lose the war. This is very true in terms of dealing with relationships. Some fight to be right at the cost of losing their entire relationship. Usually, we focus so much on winning the outside battle and being right that we forget that we are really losing the emotional war inside. In order to have emotional peace you must first win your internal battle by healing the inside. Be aware that striving for inner peace will automatically cause the Protector to engage in a fierce war against your Dreamer. The Protector won't go down without a fight. Once you create peace in your inner world, your outer world has to submit.

However, some people unconsciously at war with themselves will subconsciously attempt to start war with you in order to validate their labels and create a hostile environment. If you keep your cool and stay conscious by controlling your reaction, you will find that you always have a choice to not engage. The Protector wants you to believe that you have no other choice but to react and fight back. The truth is you can always choose to respond the right away.

There is a difference between responding and reacting. Responding takes conscious thinking about what you are feeling and doing. Reacting is when you subconsciously behave in line with the Protector's negative label of you. When you respond you have to the ability to look at the long-term damage or consequences versus the short-term satisfaction that comes from revenge. When you are conscious, you are in the Dreamer's mode: you are not triggered back to whatever year the first wound was created and you are not reacting and behaving as the wounded child.

The battle of wills is raging inside of us every day. Your emotions are an important indicator to find out the root of your problems. The decision to have an honest look under the hood of your heart is the first step toward peace and consciousness. It's a difficult road because it usually leads to digging up buried pain and opening old wounds. No one likes to revisit the past or the pain, yet in order to understand our present and our future our history will always give us a big clue. You do not want to recreate your bad history.

The reality is that we already unconsciously revisit the past whenever we are triggered, so what I am suggesting is to be present and conscious as you are triggered back to the past. This is very difficult to do on your own. At the FRESH Awareness workshops you have an opportunity to meet a team of Dreamers that can help you navigate out of the bad neighborhoods of your mind and provide you with new tools to help you be successful in your battle of wills. Nothing will change until you roll up your sleeves and take personal responsibility for your emotional well-being by taking ownership of (and applying) the new tools provided for you.

Make Taking Care of Your Heart Your First Priority

One of the saddest things that I experienced dealing with people is the way they avoid taking care of their hearts. They will use time, money, and their energy as an excuse. As you go on this journey of healing, you will get all kinds of opposition and resistance. Your time will all of a sudden start to evaporate and you'll get busy. You will want to put it off as you always have because you will believe that it's just not the right time. Your money suddenly will disappear, or you will not find enough value to invest your money on healing yourself. Remember, the outside environment has to match and feed the label you adopted. For example, the belief system that comes from the "You're not worthy to take care of your heart" label will make sure you don't have time, energy and money to change that label. If you are not aware of the root of these excuses you will give into these excuses and keep procrastinating on your healing process.

A good friend and mentor once told me that where you spend your time, money and energy is what is most important to you. Unfortunately, taking care of our hearts doesn't make the top priority list unless our emotional engine breaks down. In other words, only when the pain becomes unbearable is when you see the need for change. When you decide that you are going to get healing no matter what, you will always find the time, money and energy to get what you want. Everything in life that is worthwhile requires our time, energy and money. The door of healing is always staring you in the face, but you must walk through it. You must make it a priority to move forward with the healing you need. Think about the amount of lost time, energy and money that the grief has already caused you. Once you understand the price you are really paying for your unhealed emotions you will quickly find the time, money and energy to get the healing you need.

Don't allow the Protector to fool you. You're only guaranteed today, there is no guarantee for tomorrow. The Protector will attack your time, money, and energy because he knows these areas have the most socially acceptable excuses. The root of these excuses is attached to which voice we recognize and listen to. Once again, you must be conscious in order to make the right decision about healing. The Dreamer in you wants healing more than you do. The Protector wants your pain to grow with time, your energy to be drained with negativity, and for you to use your money to perpetuate the negative label he has of you.

Before you decide to quit your journey to healing because of these reasons or excuses, ask yourself which voice you are listening to. Is your defense mechanism activated? Are you justifying, denying, or projecting your pain? Are you rejecting the healing? What background noise are you listening to? Who is helping you translate what you are experiencing with these obstacles? Write it down. Then ask yourself what is the real fear behind these excuses. Once you get the voice of the Dreamer in place, ask your heart which is the way to go. Once you make a decision, stick to it. The saying "Where is a will there's a way" is very true of this journey.

As you have been reading this book, a light has been shed on your unconscious behavior and belief system. For that, I am very proud of you. You have invested time, money and energy so far. You've knowingly, or unknowingly, broken through resistance. Therefore I know you have it in you to break free from your emotional belief systems. Remember the small victories, like reading this far, because they will help you when you doubt and think you don't have what it takes overcome the bigger obstacles. The big victories are the accumulation of a bunch of small victories over a period of time. There is more self-discovery in this journey.

Keep up the momentum! Go on to the next chapter and continue this journey with me.

Chapter 2

RELATIONSHIP AWARENESS

The Beginning: Relationship 101

How important is it to get a real time perspective about relationships? Imagine you are on your death bed and your doctor asks you one question: Who do you want to be with you in your last hour? You would most likely say your friends or family or both. You would probably not say your car, trophies, house, bank account, or any other material things. So then why do we work and spend more time on those things than on the people we are actually providing for?

The time we spend with people we love is regulated by the time we spend providing for them. You can tell what is important to you by looking at what you spend most of your time and energy on. Unfortunately, by default, most of our time and energy is spent at our job working to pay for things we won't care about more than our family as we lay on our death bed. Does it make sense to work all your life only to come home to an empty house or a house filled with empty relationships? Many people find themselves exactly there, dying alone without real relationships. Hopefully, that will not be you!

In your defense, you may say to yourself, "I have to work in order to make a living. I can't be on the street." I am not saying to quit your job and go live on the street. I am saying to step away from your schedule and your work life for a few minutes. Imagine your life, based on what you are doing right now, and fast forward the results 10 years from now. What does that look like? It may surprise you how much time you spend on the things that are not going to matter in your dying days.

I had a friend call me for coaching in his marriage and he told me how he focused so much on his new business and decided to put his family "on hold" until he got his business profitable so he could take care of his family. When he had achieved his goal of making his business more profitable, his marriage was on the brink of divorce. He devoted more of his time, energy and heart to his work, and had nothing left over for his wife and kids. There are many stories like my friend's. It doesn't matter where you are financially; we all need balance in our lives. However, there are specific patterns of thinking that have run our lives ever since we were children regarding the importance we put on relationships.

THE ROOT

Most people go through life bearing the fruit of damaged relationships while never searching for the root of their fruit. "Make a tree good and its fruit will be good, or make a tree bad and its fruit will be bad, for a tree is recognized by its fruit." Matthew 12:33 NIV

Studies have shown that the brain remembers things that are very emotional. Whether good or bad, they imprint in our minds forever. The very first relationship I saw belonged to the people who influenced my mind the most growing up- my parents. They had a very dysfunctional relationship. At first they were in love. Then they slept in different beds. And they argued what seemed like every night. As a child this was very emotional. It was the most impactful relationship experience in my life. The brain, like a computer, stores these painful or positive memories under our "relationship" file, and as soon as we come face to face with thoughts or feelings regarding this area, our minds go back to what is imprinted in our memory.

These memories shape your relationship belief system. So your set of beliefs about your relationships are pre-programmed, ranging from your definition of what it means to be loved, to love, and even to who you should hate. Each file contains our own definitions of and belief systems surrounding trust, love, hate, communication, community, partnership, what is safe, what is functional or dysfunctional.

Most people never even ask themselves the most important question: "Where did I first learn how to be in a relationship?" They never go to the root of the problem which is where the brain began to program its knowledge about relationships. Studies have shown that between the ages of 0 and 4 years of age about 50% of the mind has already been programmed. Between 4 to 8 years of age, about 30% of the mind is programmed. And between 8-18 years of age, about 15% is programmed. So by 18 years of age our mind and emotions have already been 95% programmed. Think about it for a second. Our relationship file is almost fully established by the time we are 18 years old. When it came to any of my relationships, I was already producing results just like my mom and dad. I even started to attract relationships which resembled the programming in my mind whether it produced good or bad results.

For example, my parents argued with each other constantly. I developed an argumentative attitude and it felt normal to argue. It was the only thing my mind relied on when it came to the communication programming I set in place under my "relationship" file. I brought this set of belief systems into my marriage. My wife, however, came from the opposite spectrum. Her family life was quiet and they barely argued. Her belief system based on her relationship programming was not to argue, keep the peace at all cost, and to bury her emotions. You can imagine the contrast. We were both subconsciously trying to recreate what we believed to be normal communication based on our past programming.

My Fight to Be Right

As I said before the most impactful emotional memory originates from my past relationship growing up. As a child I saw my father and mother argue constantly. They yelled at each other all the time. No one gave in. No one apologized. They were both always right. They would argue so loudly that they would wake up the neighborhood. This was a very painful memory. The programming was, "Fight to be right." However, I didn't know that was my programming until I started to see the results I was producing in my relationships.

As an adult when I got married, our first few years were rough. Sometimes I would argue with my wife for no apparent reason. I fought with everything she said. Arguing and being loud was normal to me. It was all I was taught as a child. I was subconsciously repeating my past in attempt to fix what was shattered emotionally in my heart as a child. I created chaos so I could fix today what was broken in my past. Again, this was not done consciously; it was a reaction to a past memory. Thanks to the new programming on relationships and the support of friends, I was able to stop "Fighting to be right" about my past or trying to fix it through my wife.

Once I was coaching one of my clients who kept going from one bad relationship to another. He seemed to attract the wrong person every time. The attraction came from his belief system or programming from his past. He was subconsciously looking to recreate his past. He could not stop himself from living in dysfunction because it was all he knew. In a sense, dysfunction became functional. He was given the tools to change, but unfortunately he did not use them. Change would threaten his past which he protected at all cost. Why? He needed to be right about his past more than he wanted to change his present. It's as if he was trying to acknowledge his pain was real, and new ways of looking at the event scared him into thinking he would not have the justice that he believed was due to him. By maintaining dysfunction in his life, he was able to validate the pain of his past programming. This validation subconsciously brought him the justice he was looking for.

We're always trying to recreate our most impactful emotional memories of our past relationships. Why? We are subconsciously attempting to "fix" our past or the need to be right about our past. We won't be able to fix or heal our programming until we feel complete (or resolved) with the pain of our past. It's an impossible task if you don't know the tools to complete your past. We will talk later about the tools which will help you heal emotionally.

The Trust Programming

As a child I was abused by my father whom I loved and trusted. He took away my trust in him, but it was not just in him. It was in everyone who loved me. I began to believe that people who love me will lure me in and then pull the carpet out from under me. When someone loved me I was expecting them to hurt me. I would go back subconsciously to this emotionally painful memory and pull out a file under "Love and Trust." My mind would automatically react to my past. I would get angry and accuse the people who loved me of doing something wrong. I would look for evidence of their wrongdoing and even if I did not find anything, I would pull my heart back. Of course they would react and then that became the reason I chose to find fault in them. I would create scenarios which would trigger their belief system or file under "relationship" and cause them to react. My mind had to be right about what was in the file cabinet.

This process happens in seconds and most of the time I wasn't aware of it happening. Looking back at my relationships, I would look for the type of people who would fit the profile for a perfect match with my belief system. Remember, the Protector in you will always try to keep your belief system producing the same results, in fear of you changing the files and producing different results. How many times have you acknowledged something you did was bad for you and you promised yourself you would stop, only to find yourself repeating it the next day or the very next hour? Life is way too short to find out you could have created relationships that empower, not deplete you.

Your Sphere of Influence

"Birds of a feather flock together." – English Proverb

"Bad company corrupts good character." 1 Corinthians 15:33

Who do you surround yourself with? We will become the sum of the 5 people we surround ourselves with. Successful people will usually surround themselves with other successful people. The truth is the same goes for unsuccessful people. Misery loves company.

As I talked about before, our mind has been programmed to attract the type of relationship we filed in our memory when we were kids. So, we naturally support ourselves with people who will reinforce what we believe about ourselves. The strongest belief you have of yourself will also lead you to search for people who will support that belief. The more you surround yourself with a certain group of people the more you become like them. You adapt to your environment. Still need more evidence of the fact that we become like the people we hang out with the most? Have you ever heard yourself talk like a friend of

41

yours whom you talk to all the time? Have you ever started using the same words they use? We all have. How about our parents? Do you talk like your parents and yes, even worse, act like them as much as you said you wouldn't?

If you choose to take an honest look at who you are allowing to influence your life and who you are surrounding yourself with, you may or may not like the results you find. We not only need to change to our new belief system which supports us, but we also need a team of people who can support us in our new belief system. In other words, it is very essential that your environment supports your new belief so it can grow.

Once you become aware of the relationships that are not helpful you are usually faced with two main reactions: 1) Fear of being left alone, or 2) blaming others for your surroundings.

#1 Fear Of Being Left Alone

Let's start with fear of being alone. The fear of being left behind is what most people think about once they realize their circle of influence is not helping them grow but actually reinforcing a belief system which doesn't create the results they would like. This fear is usually covered up by fear of rejection when you shift your circle of influence. I am not saying to just stop hanging out with your friends who are not successful in the areas you want to be. I am saying to limit the time you spend with people who are going in a direction that is the opposite of who you want to become. Here is the solution to the problem: Make new friends who will support the person you are trying to become.

I once heard a Chinese Proverb that goes something like this, "Give a man a fish and you feed him for a day; Teach a man to fish and you feed him for a lifetime." I'd rather have a friend who teaches me how to fish than a friend who gives me a fish for a day. What do I mean by that? A friend who gives you a fish is only doing what his friends or family has taught him. Now why would a friend give you a fish for a day, which does not help you in the long run? They are experts at taking care of the short term results in your life, financially, spiritually, emotionally, health-wise, and in your relationships. Most don't do it out of malice since it's all they have been taught. For example, someone who has been single all their lives and wants to keep being single will not teach you how to be married. He will give you a fish for the day. He can only teach you what he knows: a single lifestyle. The same is true for the rest of the areas of your life. The ones who teach you to fish are the ones who empower you to change. They are always calling you higher. They also

43

a support system to help you
ιe the fear of change. They are the
and the leaders who themselves
e.

#2 Blaming Others

The second most common reaction to
becoming aware of your surrounding is
blaming others. We become angry at the
people we surrounded ourselves with
because we see them as people who are
holding us back. We then become indignant
with them. We may be saying to ourselves
"Look at the people I surround myself with!
No wonder I am where I am in life. They
are so negative." We can then come across
self-righteous and of course our circle of
influence will reject us. Remember who
actually chose these friends in the first
place. Yep. You guessed it: YOU.

Another set of emotions can come into
play when the people we surround
ourselves with are not successful in the
areas where we lack success. Then we start
to feel helpless like there is no one around
who can help. I have felt like that before. I
have felt as if I had been left alone in my
quest to make a change in my life and that
people gave up on me or looked down on
me. The truth is that most people think
about themselves before others. Most

people judge others based on the way they view themselves and blame others more than taking responsibility for their own actions. So I started to complain about "Most people." I realized when I complained about "most people" that I actually became like them. Whenever we complain or act like a victim we become like those we are complaining about.

Nothing will change unless the person in the mirror looking back at you decides to change. You get what you put out. You actually repel people who are able to help you when you are in a complaining or victim mode. The minute I started taking personal responsibility for my lack of relationships with mentors, I began to attract personal coaches. I believe they were there all along but I was not ready to receive their help yet. In the same way, when you take responsibility for your contribution to your problems and your response to your problems or whatever you are complaining about, you will also begin to attract solutions and the help you need. It's no coincidence that you picked up this book. Something inside you attracted you here. This could mean you are ready for a change. As the saying goes, "when the student is ready, the teacher will appear" (Buddhist Proverb).

Relationship Communication Styles

You have heard the phrase, "win-win situation." It is usually used in some sort of sales context. What you do not hear is, "I have a win-lose deal for you." That won't get you lots of customers or friends for that matter. What does it mean to have a win-win situation? It's when both parties involved win in the end. It's when everyone wins. I will share with you a situation that happened to me when I went to a mechanic. I have been going to this mechanic for years but something happened over the years. He started charging me more than what I thought it should cost. Yet based on trust I kept taking my car in and getting ripped off. However, I didn't feel as confident as I used to feel in referring my friends to this mechanic.

One day another friend of mine told me about this other mechanic who is very honest with his prices and does a fantastic job, but very cheap. At first I did not trust this new guy even though he had worked on another neighbor's car for 20 years and he had fixed my friend's car at a very low price. I questioned why his price was so low and the integrity of his work. So the next time my car needed something minor to be fixed, I still took it to my mechanic- the one I was used to. Well, once again he charged me another exorbitant amount which did not feel right. Soon, my wife's car needed a brake job and some maintenance work. I had no choice but to give this new guy a try. I remembered the words of Chinese proverb "Fool me once, shame on you; Fool me twice, shame on me". The outcome was that this new guy charged me the best price ever and I even felt compelled to give him a tip. And the work he did was excellent.

Now how long do you think I am going to go to my 1st mechanic? That's WIN-LOSE. He won my money but I felt a loss because of the price and service I received. How about my 2nd mechanic? That is what you call a WIN-WIN.

He won because he got a new, satisfied and loyal customer. And I felt like I won because of the price and service I got. The 1st Mechanic ultimately LOST because he lost a customer and many more referrals. The 2nd Mechanic ultimately WON big time because he not only got a new customer but a bunch of referrals from me. So what does this have to do with win-win communication? The attitude you have with your Relationships (WIN–LOSE or WIN-WIN) is directly related to your style of communication. Let's take a look at the 4 types of relationship communication:

1. *LOSE–WIN = LOSE (My voice doesn't matter) INDEPENDENT*

2. *WIN-LOSE = LOSE (I take over the conversation. Only my voice matters) INDEPENDENT*

3. *LOSE-LOSE = LOSE (No one is being real) CODEPENDENT*

4. *WIN-WIN = WIN (Listen twice as much as I speak) INTERDEPENDENT*

If you are thinking only of getting, not giving, then your style is WIN-LOSE. In Marriage people will win the fight to prove their point at the expense of their spouse's wellbeing. Your spouse becomes your enemy. "If she could only be more like me," is a WIN-LOSE statement because she will lose herself to you. She will lose who she is to become more like you. In short, as Stephen R. Covey said, a "Seek first to understand, then to be understood" attitude will get you to a WIN-WIN situation.

The same principle applies to our relationship with children. Not letting your child express how they feel is a WIN-LOSE situation because the only one who expresses themselves is the parent. I am not saying you can't express yourself but we must let children express themselves also. The children face the same problem. If you are letting them do all the expressing and you are not expressing yourself, then that is also a LOSE-WIN situation. Remember a WIN-WIN is when BOTH parties feel like they have won.

How about with our friends? How does this apply? Have you ever heard the saying, "What goes around comes around" or "You reap what you sow"? That is the formula for either a WIN-WIN or a LOSE-LOSE relationship. Here is an example: When you are gossiping about your friend, you may feel that you are winning but someone else will for sure gossip about you. Then you will realize that it was LOSE-LOSE. In friendship the person who consistently takes is losing. It may look like WIN-LOSE but in the end it becomes a LOSE-WIN. On the other hand, the person who consistently allows others to run over them is engaging in a LOSE-WIN.

When you are refreshing others you automatically refresh yourself. The more you respect and honor others, the more you will receive respect and honor. You may not receive it from everyone you give it to, but it will come from a different source. Choosing not to engage or give in to toxic communication is honoring yourself and the other person. As long as you respect and honor everyone, including yourself, and live in integrity with yourself and how you communicate, you WIN! This still is WIN-WIN communication, because how you respond is not dependent on how others respond.

In conclusion, WIN-LOSE and LOSE-WIN both end up as LOSE-LOSE. There is a communication style most people love the most. Despite its destructive power, it doesn't seem to bother most people and is actually a socially acceptable form of communication. It feels like a WIN-LOSE but it's really a LOSE-LOSE. This style is one of the top relationship killers It is gossip.

Gossip Separates Close Friends

Gossip is like an infection. Left untreated it grows more and more. It leads to judgment and destruction of relationships. So why do we gossip? When I have gossiped it made me feel better about myself. Have you ever talked about someone and they happened to hear what you said? Or have you ever spoken about someone and then found yourself making sure you really hung up the phone so they won't hear? What is gossip?

Gossip is when you are talking about someone's private issues without their permission to someone who has nothing to do with the situation. You are not building someone up. You are tearing them down. They might have hurt you, so you call it venting. Let me be clear on this subject. Unless you have a genuine concern for the other person and you are genuinely interested and already in a position to ask how to help that person, then, in my opinion, you are gossiping. For example, if someone tells you they are thinking of hurting themselves or someone else, they require help. If you share this with someone in a position to give that help, this is not gossip. You'll know when you gossip because you'll want to justify it right after you do it or while you're doing it. You'll be almost complaining about the other person's personal issue. You usually gossip to someone who can't help the situation or to someone who won't help your view on the person you're talking about. Remember, the person who is gossiping to you has probably already gossiped or will gossip about you.

How does gossip separate close friends? Imagine someone who is very close to you talks about you behind your back and you find out about it. You will probably not want to share any other information with that person. You will most likely not want to be around that person anymore and lose all trust in them. Now the relationship that was once close becomes a distant acquaintance or an enemy.

"If Only They Could Do It My Way!"

Have you ever thought that way? What cracks me up the most is when I see myself and almost everyone else around me complaining after they see a bad movie. We complain about how we could have done a better job. We have no clue what it takes to make a movie but we could do a better job just because our way is the best! I am not saying there aren't bad movies out there, but my point is that it takes a lot of money, people, time, coordination and lots of stuff we can't even imagine to put a movie together! We all have the natural tendency to think we can do a better job than someone else. We are always justifying ourselves to make ourselves look good. This type of thinking shows up the most in relationships.

I had a friend once who complained about his spouse. He went on for an hour about the reason why he felt he was right about a fight they had. He went on and on about how wrong she was. He mentioned to me, "if only she could respect me the same way I respect her." He felt he deserved to be respected because of his deeds. He worked very hard for his family to provide a roof and food on the table. He did not feel appreciated by his wife.

I asked him, "What does she want you to work on?"

He replied, "She wants me to connect with her emotionally by actively listening and validating her."

I then asked him, "Would that make her feel loved?"

He replied, "Yes."

Then I asked, "Do you give her that emotional connection she is asking for?"

His reply: "I am trying....but ......" In other words, the answer was "NO."

We want our spouse or friends to be more like us or do things our way but we are not willing to do the same thing they ask of us. This situation is one that I encounter in myself and a lot of people I meet all the time. Most people want something they aren't willing to give so they fight tooth and nail to get it. But sometimes winning the fight means losing the battle. Both people sit on opposite ends of the couch not talking to each other and instead focus on how the other is wrong. Who actually wins? No one wins, because no one is willing to seek to understand. Most of us seek only to be understood and then forget about the other's feelings.

How Do We Improve Our Relationships?

I believe one of the most common problems in relationships is passivity. The dictionary definition of passivity is the trait of remaining inactive; a lack of initiative. In a relationship, passivity happens when one person stops working on bettering themselves and as a result cannot contribute to the betterment of the relationship. I don't believe that being passive comes from us making a conscious decision. I believe it's a learned behavior. I personally learned this behavior from my parents who went from being active in their marriage to becoming passive. They didn't invest in their marriage the way they did in the beginning. Once they became passive in their marriage they became frustrated with each other and started to look for love outside their marriage.

At times passivity starts when we stop trying, because we want someone else to come rescue us or do the work for us. We start to expect positive results in a relationship without putting effort to improve it. You also might have learned this behavior growing up. For example, if you had a parent who did everything for you as a child, now as an adult you might be subconsciously expecting someone else to do the same. On the opposite end of the spectrum you might have had a parent who didn't do anything for you, but now you are still looking for someone to give you the care you never had growing up. These parents were still passive when it came to taking care of your emotional needs. The first part of figuring out a solution is to be aware that you have a problem. The history of your patterns will lead you to the root of where you learned to be passive. However, regardless of where your behavior comes from, passivity will remain unless we consciously change our behavior. When we see the pain created in ourselves and others by our passivity, change will eventually follow.

What does being passive produce? Your passivity in a relationship may produce anger, resentment, and/or envy. Your anger may come from the feeling of entitlement; wanting someone to do for us what we won't do for them. Resentment soon follows when you begin to focus on the other person's lack of engagement as you become self-righteous about your own progress. In order words, you may be thinking that people are not moving or growing fast enough for you. The envy is when you see the grass greener on the other side of the fence (in other relationships). You may start to compare your spouse or partner with someone else or other relationships that seem to have it all together. In addition to all this, passivity will produce a lack of muscle in the persevering and personal growth department.

When a caterpillar is in a cocoon it has to use its strength and aggressively use its wings to break out of that shell. This process strengthens its wings so it can have the strength to fly. If this process of being aggressive and persevering is interrupted by someone else who wants to "help" the butterfly to break out of its cocoon, it could kill the butterfly. How? The butterfly will not have the strength to fly and will eventually fall to the ground and die. When you are passive and not aggressive, you are not using the muscles you need to persevere and help your relationship progress to the next level. The death of that relationship is inevitable. It could be the death of the passion in that relationship or even the death of the relationship itself.

Why do we not put the effort we need to have the relationship we want? Once, again it is based on our belief systems that we have learned growing up. As I mentioned before, we want someone to rescue us. We don't want to work at our relationship but we expect the full reward. I have seen couples learn powerful tools and start to change but then become comfortable and become passive. It's very easy to see this process when a couple is dating, at first, there's romance is in the air, then they may even get married. After the first few years of marriage they go from being aggressively giving to each other to passively living together. They stop doing what they did at first to keep the romance in the air. They have forgotten the Law of Reaping and Sowing. The law simply states that you get what you put in. So don't expect to get what you don't put in.

What's the solution to passivity? Have you ever taken the time to notice how a butterfly flies? It makes it look so easy! To think that this beautiful creature could have died because of its lack of perseverance is tragic. We all have to aggressively grow in our love, before we can fly like that butterfly in our relationships. We can't expect to want something for nothing. Even if you could get something for nothing you wouldn't be as grateful for it. Be aggressive in working on improving yourself more than your partner.

In the Emotional Awareness chapter, I spoke of the Protector wanting the opposite of what's good for you. Passivity is what he uses to drain the hope of change in a relationship. As the Protector uses time, money and energy as an excuse for you not to invest in dealing with healing your emotions, he will use the same areas to make you give in to passivity. Many people say they are too tired, or overwhelmed to deal with getting help or going to a relationship workshop on improving their relationship. These are the very people who have the most horrific relationships. On the other hand the people who invest time, money and energy in their relationship usually have a healthy relationship.

The Dreamer in you wants you to aggressively embrace personal growth, because he knows it keeps the hope that things can change in your relationships. The Protector's purpose is to bring death to anything that might produce genuine love. The best way to do that is to kill any hope of a better future or change in your relationships. Once your hope is gone, you will eventually give up fighting for your relationship. The Dreamer, on the other hand, has a purpose to spark life and hope in your relationship. If you find your relationship stagnate, ask yourself who became passive. And before you point the finger to your partner, take a good look at areas of your life that you allowed yourself to become passive. Many times, there may be a separate area of your life that you left unchecked and became passive. That area will affect other areas of your life.

For example, being passive in dealing with your past emotional scars will indirectly affect how you give yourself in your current relationship. If you want to improve your relationship, you must search for the areas of your life where you allowed yourself to become passive. When you are consistently aggressive in creating the type of relationship you want, you will be aware of the other areas of your life where you are passive.

So let's review some steps on how to aggressively go after improving your relationships:

1. *Go to the Root of the Problem.* (Your belief system you programmed as a child)

2. *Find a healthy role model.* (Reprogramming the file under Relationships) Find someone (or couples) in a sphere of influence who will tell you the truth about you and will help you to become more unified in your relationship. Look for someone who exemplifies the type of relationship you want and follow their steps.

3. *Ask for help.* There is something magical

that happens when you are feeling like you are the only one on earth going through your relationship problem and then you talk to someone else and they say "I have been there and done that and it's going to be ok." Even just being vulnerable with your partner by asking for their help and support can break down their defense mechanism. Express your true needs versus your anger that your needs are not being met.

4. *Review your communication style.* Is it a WIN-WIN? Become a better listener. Ask yourself what steps am I going to take to become a better listener in my relationships?

5. *Don't quit being aggressive about improving yourself in the relationship.* Many times we give up on ourselves and/or on our partner just when we are about to turn a corner. We can't expect overnight success. We also can't expect a fulfilling relationship without putting in the effort.

There is an important item in the relationship that I will talk about in the chapter on spirituality. I will share with you the most important glue that is actively keeping my marriage together now going over a decade.

You're doing well in your journey! Let's continue your self-discovery by turning the page to the next chapter.

Chapter 3

FINANCIAL AWARENESS

The SELF-WORTH Trigger

"Your self-worth is not your net worth." ~Anonymous

I had heard that saying many times in many different ways over the years, but I never really got the full meaning of it until I started looking at the attachment I had with my net worth. Like most people, I have a negative net worth. This doesn't mean that I view myself as less valuable as an individual than other people. Instead, it quite literally means that my debts and liabilities have generally exceeded my income and assets. I don't think I'm very different from most other people who don't really think much about their net worth unless it's in the positive. As I write this, the US is in debt to the tune of trillions of dollars. There is a growing number of job loss and incredible instability in the business environment. This leaves people thinking more about their debt than their self-worth. Yet, if we focus more on understanding our <u>self</u>-worth, we can actually overcome our negative <u>net</u> worth.

Perhaps the reason we do not understand the phrase "your self-worth is not your net worth" is because we don't fully understand the definition of "worth". The Webster Dictionary definition of the word worth is "the quality that renders something desirable, useful, or valuable." Most people equate their self-worth with the amount of money in their bank account or the volume of personal material possessions. The unfortunate by-product of such thinking is that we to turn the power to increase or decrease our self-worth over to our money and possessions. This is not foreign to us — who hasn't known a person who cannot seem to disconnect their wardrobe, their home, their vehicle or other possessions from their definition of their self-worth? Maybe you have seen this person in the mirror.

When I look around, I see that we live in a society that is more concerned about outward appearances than inward virtues. Recently, I went to a business meeting with an individual who had an undeniable "look-at-me" attitude. I could easily tell that outward appearance was very important to him, but with a little discernment I could also sense that this outward conceit covered up a deep inward insecurity. Is looking good on the outside a bad thing? Not at all. However, when outward appearances begin to define our self-esteem, then a danger appears. But deep inside we know that it's a losing battle. Everything you have, including your good looks, eventually fades away.

Self-worth has nothing to do with what we drive or wear, but our "look good" mental programming says it does. What is a "look good" programming? It's what society programmed in your mind since you were a child: In order to be accepted, your outward appearance is of greatest importance. Where does this programming come from? People generally experience this cultural imprint between birth and 18 years of age. Remember how the "cool" kids in school attracted so much attention with their looks? For any reader who is a parent, you know how much more the intensity of style, fashion, and toys can be for our children than it was for previous generations. Most people's conversation begins with a greeting by asking a person's name. Usually, the next question is "What do you do"? We are programmed to focus on "self-worth is your net worth". The media bombards us with the supposed importance of outside appearance. The tragedy is that in our society we grow up attempting to increase our self-worth with material things. This causes us to become so attached to material satisfaction that when we lose it, we become depressed to the point of despair and in some cases, to the point of suicide.

I remember when I was 25 years old I skipped going out on a date to clean my car. I idolized my car to the point of going on a date with my car versus an actual person. That night I spent cleaning and polishing my car from the inside out. I even cleaned the engine with Armor All. The next day I had a business appointment about an hour's drive away so I took off on the freeway riding on my newly detailed car. As I was driving something strange happened; I saw my hood moving abnormally. Before I could slow down my hood flipped open, smashed my front windshield and dented the top of my car. I remember being in complete disbelief as I pulled over. (It was a godsend that there was not much traffic.) When I thought carefully about this event I came up with a meaning of it: "I worshiped a car therefore God smashed it". Was God really smashing my car so I would focus on Him?

The point is not to discern whether there was divine intervention in this event, but what the effect of its meaning had on me. The pendulum swung in my mind. Previously, I had worshiped my car. After the accident, I became frustrated and distraught to the point of disregarding the care of my car. This was because of the meaning I placed on my accident: My status symbol was damaged, therefore my self-worth was damaged. My habit of extremism flung from selfish pride to self victimization. I thought I was in control, but this belief was smashed along with my car when God allowed the hood to fly off on the freeway. I didn't get mad at God, but I did walk around in "sackcloth & ashes". I had equated my car with my self-worth so when it was damaged I felt like the scum of the earth. When you feel like scum, you're not likely to care about anything, even those things that had been special to you before.

Where did it all begin? The Bible states that mankind is made in God's image. Yet mankind, generally, is either unwilling or unable to grasp this concept. As a result, we allow our material possessions to define who we are. We can't get past this "look good" programming, especially because materialism is rampant in our society. I believe it started all the way back to Genesis when Adam and Eve bit into the forbidden fruit from the tree of the Knowledge of Good & Evil. In Genesis 1:25 it says "Now both the man and his wife were both naked, but they felt no shame". Their "look good" programming was not active yet. They didn't care about what the other person thought about them. Their outward appearance didn't matter because they were secure in God. However, right after they ate the fruit the Scripture says "At that moment their eyes were opened, and they suddenly felt shame at their nakedness. So they sewed fig leaves together to cover themselves" (Genesis 3:7). The "look good" programming was born as the first piece of clothing was made because of shame. Thousands of years later the clothing industry is a billion dollar industry. According to a study done at North Dakota State University in 2010, the average American spends roughly $2000 on clothes every year[3]. Clothing is not the only thing we can use to cover up our shame in order to "look good". We can also use other material possessions. We do this when we have low self esteem, and low self-worth to cover up our insecurities.

What Shall We Do Then?

Am I saying to wear shabby clothes and be careless with our possessions? No, not at all. I understand we are in a society that places enormous emphasis on looks, and in some ways our outward appearance indicates how we feel about ourselves internally. We can't change the world but we can choose not to attach our self-worth to our net worth or appearance. In the book The Millionaire Next Door a study was done regarding today's millionaire class. It turns out that most of those millionaires drive pickup trucks and buy suits for less than $500 which they buy at an average department store.

[3] Information found on TLC website
http://tlc.howstuffworks.com/family/average-family-spend-on-clothing.htm in the article, titled *What does the average family spend on clothing?* by Emilie Sennebogen

Warren Buffet, one of the richest men in the world, still lives in the same home he bought after he first got married about 50 years ago. Not only does he still live in this modest home, but he also drives his own car and does not have security guards around him. He doesn't have anything to prove. You may be saying, "If I had all the money in the world I wouldn't have anything to prove either." The person you are now will be the same person with more money. Money doesn't change your heart but in fact money reveals your true character. If you are generous with a small amount of money you will also be generous with a large amount of money. The opposite is true: If you are greedy with the money you have now, then you'll be greedy when you get more money.

Choosing of Financial Lifestyle

Everyone chooses their own financial lifestyle they want to live whether poor, middle class, or rich. These choices are mostly influenced by our early programming (e.g., our parents) and our social programming. Once we choose our financial lifestyle we surround ourselves with people around us who would support that lifestyle. We are usually not happy with our financial situation because we feel that it chose us rather than accepting that we chose it. Finding out where the mentality comes from is essential to changing it.

In the face of all kinds of problems, we all too often focus on our desired outcome without looking at the foundation of the problem. In financial matters, we are likely to build our life by going after material goods, which are superficial, without building a foundation of fiscal responsibility. This is profound. We have been programmed from birth regarding financial matters, whether we know it or not, which means that as we grow older we choose our lifestyle based on that programming.

We may claim to want financial stability, but our pursuit of material success over spiritual application of financial management shows something else. Action speaks louder than words. We must then repeatedly ask ourselves: Am I happy with the choice I've made so far for my financial lifestyle?

The Trap

There is an interesting story on how some natives learned to catch a spider monkey. By sheer natural speed capabilities, spider monkeys are too fast to catch, but the natives used their ingenuity to trap these speedy critters. They would put food in a jar with a trick opening big enough for the spider monkey to fit his hand in, but which would not be big enough to pull his hand out. The spider monkey would come down from their trees and in their haste to grab the food they would get stuck. The spider monkey would drag this jar around making it impossible to climb trees or run fast enough to escape. That's when the natives would be able to catch them. The fate of any spider monkey caught this way was not positive.

A friend of mine has been working as employee for other people all his life. He was presented with a business partnership opportunity in a highly productive industry, and there was a significant opportunity to make money. He was aware that his employer was laying off employees to cut costs, and there was a great chance he too would be downsized out of a job. By all estimates, there was a 90 percent chance of success in this venture. Yet he struggled fiercely with whether or not he should take this opportunity based on the 10 percent risk factor.

My friend was so used to the illusion of job security that, even though he knew that job security as he had known it historically no longer existed, he opted to hold on to his day job and pass on the business partnership. My friend was not happy with his choice, but he could not overcome his programming to take a calculated risk where the payoff could have been a great boost to his pocketbook and his spirit.

The things we hold on to when we are afraid to let go can get us killed in the end. My friend's job was not bad but it was his spider monkey jar. There was no way he could race after a new opportunity, because he could not break himself free from the jar.

What is the solution for fear of the unknown? Wisdom. My friend was advised to pray for wisdom because God will grant it to those who truly seek it. I believe God can change your "thinking" about money, and will replace such thinking with His wisdom. The only difference between the "Haves" and the "Have-Not's" is their way of thinking, their wisdom. You can have two people holding a dollar but what they do with that dollar makes the difference. The dollar does not discriminate. We all have 24 hours in a day. Time also does not discriminate. Yet what we do with that dollar and that time keeps us where we are in our chosen lifestyle.

The Choice

I just came from a house in Beverly Hills with a tennis court and pool sitting on half an acre of land. I was amazed by the difference that I saw driving from Beverly Hills to a "regular" neighborhood. The houses, cars, and restaurants are significantly more plush in a place like Beverly Hills than a typical American community. As I pulled up at the light I started to think. Why is there such a big gap between Beverly Hills — the home of the rich — and Anytown, USA — the home of the poor? I believe it is due to the fact that the rich chose their wealth both consciously and subconsciously, and the poor chose their poverty in the same way.

There have been many books written about what "secrets" the rich possess that make them who they are. The irony in this is that if we who are not rich believe that there is some magical secret to wealth and economic success the greater the gap between the common man and the rich actually becomes. We can fall into a victim mentality when we feel there is a mystery to become wealthy. There is no mystery or short cut to get to the other side — it starts with a mindset that believes in and goes after wealth.

How do we choose the financial lifestyle we have? The choice is made in the way we earn, spend, invest, and save money. When we know we shouldn't be spending on something of little value yet we make such a purchase, we have made decision subconsciously to be poor. When we get up every day like clockwork to punch a clock for someone else hoping an opportunity for something better to come along, we are subconsciously choosing to be an employee. Later in this chapter, I will be discussing the habits which keep us in our chosen financial lifestyle and how to switch them.

The Lion Never Sleeps

The subconscious is very powerful. It's our belief system: our programming. It never sleeps, and in fact it works while we sleep. I think of the subconscious mind as an automatic transmission. The gears automatically changes without you really physically changing them. It's done for you as you rev up to whatever speed you choose. Habits become subconscious; you are not actively thinking about what you are doing. I believe we in America have put our financial minds on automatic, on cruise control. In our fleeting emotions, we would like to speed up our financial security, yet our subconscious mind still changes the spending gears for us unknowingly. The more we make the more we spend automatically. Many people feel like they're in control of their finances and that they're going somewhere when in fact they're going nowhere fast. Their subconscious mind has their financial life on automatic.

The conscious mind is like a stick shift, or manual transmission, car. It operates much the same as an automatic car but we are in control of when to shift it. If we don't shift properly the car starts to sputter and stall. We know which gear we are in because we can feel and hear the car's engine. Awareness of self is the conscious mind. When we are aware of our financial choices we will be able to shift into a new gear at the right time. It is more difficult and takes more effort to learn to drive a manual transmission than an automatic. When learning how to operate a stick shift, one has to figure out just the right balance of gas and clutch needed to effectively maneuver the vehicle. It is not natural at first. It is a new skill. However after learning it you get so used to it that driving a stick shift becomes practically as simple as automatic. I believe it's the same progression when we are learning a new financial skill or belief system. We are so accustomed to being automatic that we have forgotten that we are the ones in charge of changing our financial gears.

How to Change From an Automatic to a "Stick Shift" Financial Lifestyle: Awareness

The very first thing is to be aware of the type of lifestyle you are choosing for yourself. Are you an automatic or a manual transmission, stick shift? The best way to answer that is to look at your financial condition right now. What you are spending, how you are spending it, and why you spend at all, will help you identify whether you are in control of your financial condition or whether you're on autopilot.

Whatever you are committed to will always show up in the end results of your efforts. Go back to the root of where you gained your belief system as I suggested earlier. Once you identify the roots of your belief system, there you will find the habits. The triggers are what connect you to your belief system or programming which then leads to a memory. The memory then will cause an emotional charge and an action or reaction will flow. A habit is born when this process repeats itself.   As an old Russian proverb says, "Repetition is the mother of all learning".

Identify Your Trigger

A trigger is the pull mechanism that causes a gun to fire.   For the purposes of this study (particularly your finances), the trigger is the emotional reaction or charge that causes you to spend, buy, lose, save, and invest money. When a conversation turns to money or when you have money in your possession, are your thoughts about it positive or negative? What does your emotional memory trigger you to do? Write down your emotional memory regarding money. Ask yourself: "When I was growing up, did I develop a sense that money was good or bad?

This is where the belief system is hiding.   Your memory of how you have historically handled money is what produces a belief system. Perhaps your strongest memory is that of a parent saying something negative like "You know, money doesn't grow on trees" or "Money is the root of all evil".   What they said or did with money impacted you and created an emotional memory. Your memory of the emotional events related to money created a meaning you chose to believe. That belief system is filed deep into your memory. Once the belief system is there it will ultimately produce results in your life. It's like a planted seed. With water, the seed sprouts into a plant. Whether it is a destructive weed or a lovely flower depends not on the water now, but on the nature of the original seed planted back then.

-Actions Or Habits

The belief system you created produces an action or a reaction. That action or reaction repeated over and over becomes a habit. Your subconscious mind is where your belief system dwells. Because it exists relatively unnoticed in our consciousness, the power of the subconscious is far stronger than we realize. It is our subconscious that propels our actions; actions create results; results reinforce our belief system, which then propels us back into the same pattern of behavior again. Remember: What you think or believe, so you become. Thoughts that lead to action turn your belief system into your reality. How do you find out your belief system? Follow the fruit to the root. If you look closely enough, the results (fruit) of your actions or choices will always lead you back to your belief system (root). I will go into more detail on different types of habits, both positive and negative, later in this chapter.

-Results (Or The Fruit)

Action produces results. Not taking action produces a different set of results. We are always taking some kind of action, which means we are always producing results. Stop right now and try going one second without thinking or feeling. Not easy to do, is it? Making a decision not to take action is still an action. You're always in action. The question is not whether you are in action, but what results your action produces.

-Regret Or Satisfaction

Our behavior brings us either satisfaction or regret. Satisfaction is contentment with our results, while regret is discontentment with our results. The latter is a state in our subconscious mind telling us that something is wrong and needs to change. If we are sensitive to our regrets and choose not to ignore them, we will become sick and tired of being sick and tired and will decide to change. If we numb out or dwell on our past, we have chosen the same path we've been on and resigned ourselves to more and more of the same mediocrity. Most people talk about how they wish they would have done things differently while never taking any action towards change.

-Justification

This is where the cycle begins and ends, where you cultivate your programming, and usually the area where people come close to achieving a breakthrough, but end up talking themselves out of it. It could be the "end zone" (for a glorious touchdown), but it turns out to be the quitting zone. Most people continually ask themselves "Why are things the way they are in my life?" Though some are unwilling to do more than ask that question, I have known many people who can accurately answer it. But I believe that the follow up question is just as important: "Will I do something about it?"

You can be filled with knowledge and tools for change, yet remain stuck. Remaining stuck is actually a self-justification for not making the effort to change. Have we not seen people chase after knowledge claiming that knowledge will solve their problems, but are no different after they have filled their minds with that knowledge? Such people effectively use knowledge to justify why they are not taking action. Knowledge without action is like tossing pennies into a fountain. Wishful thinking will produce as many results as that coin soaking at the bottom of the tank.

This cycle will stop when you decide to make it stop. The more aware you are of your belief system and take deliberate actions to change it, the more it becomes a habit. Once your actions become a habit, eventually your results will change. The results are the fruit of changing your habits.

To increase our awareness, let's explore some of the habits that can be produced by these different belief systems.

New Habits Start With Consistency

Habit: 1. A recurrent, often unconscious pattern of behavior that is acquired through frequent repetition. An established disposition of the mind or character. 2. Customary manner or practice. ~ (The American Heritage Dictionary)

Our belief systems create either negative habits or positive habits. They can push us to develop negative habits and create financial inconsistency in our lives.

I recently read an article on consistency by Darren Hardy titled *How to WIN – Every Time!* To quote Mr. Hardy:

> *"I used to get frustrated when I would start
> a new venture and I'd see the competition leap
> out in front and get off to a fast and successful
> start. Then I found the single discipline that*

gives me the advantage to beat anybody at almost anything – CONSISTENCY.

A lot of people become gung-ho about new goals or achievements, and they charge out of the gate in an explosion of activity – but their intensity and commitment quickly fizzle. Meanwhile, those who begin the journey with less flash but a greater commitment to consistency eventually catch up to their flamboyant peers and leave them in the dust. Do what most people don't: Stay consistent."

Consistency in our endeavors is the real-life version of the story of the tortoise and the hare. This moral fable plays out every day in the financial realm of our lives. The tortoise was slow and consistent. The hare shot out of the box with all his speed, full of confidence that he would easily beat the tortoise. But that confidence quickly turned to overconfidence. He chose to slow down and stop his sprint in favor of a leisurely rest. Meanwhile, the tortoise never stopped. He kept going because he had one thing in mind...finish the race. The victory of the tortoise was against all odds, but it wasn't speed that won the race. The win came about because of the consistency in the behavior of the tortoise. He took it one step at a time.

The Great Wall of China is well over 3,000 miles long. It is a massive construction built in a time when the only power available to the workers was a combination of their own blood, sweat, and tears. This great monument did not just appear overnight; it was built brick by brick over the course of many years. In like manner, your financial goals will be constructed like the Great Wall: one brick at the time. Everything you do today serves as a brick in your wall and affects your financial future in a good or a bad way. Every new habit you build moves you closer to your goal or pushes you farther away from it. If you have destructive habits, fear not. You can create new habits that will improve your consistency.

When my father was doing well economically, he would spend money faster than he earned it. We would go from rich to poor on a weekly basis. Feast today...famine tomorrow. Having lived in an economic whirlwind as a child created in me an emotional memory regarding finances. That emotional memory fostered my financial belief system, which in turn produced my habits with money. Since the "apple doesn't fall far from the tree", I became just like my father. When I began to earn money, I spent it quickly and with reckless abandon. While I hope it's not true, I would guess that most of my readers can relate in a very real sense to my story.

The Negative Habits of Our Financial Belief System

That being said, let's discuss some negative habits that keep us from achieving our financial goals:

HABIT #1 Quitting Too Early

This is when you close to accomplishing your goals and then pull back or when you come up to a breakthrough and get back in to your comfort zone. For Example: Working out. Pushing through your pain builds muscle. The strain the weightlifter undergoes tears at his muscles, but in the healing process rebuilds the muscle even stronger. If he quits before the burn, his strength is not enhanced. No pain no gain.

HABIT #2 "Checking Out" of Reality

In challenging situations, people all too often "check out" of reality by focusing on non-productive activities such as gossiping on the phone for hours to friends, surfing the net, playing video games, shopping, and zoning out in front of the TV.

HABIT #3 Scarcity Thinking

Scarcity thinking (also known as "Poverty Mindset" which is the belief that you do not have sufficient resources) convinces many people not to take action. Phrases like "I don't have money to do this and that" — whether actually true or not — stop people from putting plans into action that would in fact produce money for them. This is a major lie that I chose to believe over and over again which produced a habit of shutting down possibility.

HABIT #4 Pleasure vs. Investment

An "I deserve to have it" attitude — even if it's the fruit of hard work — is merely a justification for a lack of patience. Being quick to spend your earnings on the pleasure of today will leave you with no money to invest in the future. How tragic it is that all too often we must ask ourselves why we miss great investment opportunities! This cycle will not stop until we curb our appetite for spending now and allow ourselves to hunger a little longer now in exchange for something better at a later time.

HABIT #5 Blame Shifting

Most people did not have good financial role models growing up. We may not have a mentor (or even think to get one) to help us with our current economic situation. The tendency is to get frustrated because no one is there to coach us into financial freedom, so we blame people for not being there. We blame the economy, our parents, the government, and our friends. This type of self-victimization thinking only perpetuates a lack of personal responsibility for our own current situation. The truth is we subconsciously or consciously choose not get help because of the previous habits we created: Habits #1-4. We sit comfortably on these habits which are killing us slowly and make us unteachable. It's like sitting underwater, breathing slowly and hoping we will not drown.

HABIT #6 Holding Back (Not Giving 100%)

Many of us do not give a 100% effort because of an underlying fear of failure. Our results will show how much we truly put into something to make it happen. We reap what we sow. Holding back our heart is like dipping your toes in the water for a long time before jumping in, but ultimately choosing not to swim. It's playing not to lose versus playing to win. It's not setting high expectations so you won't be disappointed. It's waiting until the last minute to try to reach your goal. It's not working every day towards the goal and yet expecting results that only come from 100% daily effort.

The Positive Habits of Our Financial Belief System

Now, let's explore some belief systems that create positive habits.

My father, in spite of some of his Negative Habits, was a successful entrepreneur. He took a big risk when he took off from the US to go start a business in Africa where he didn't even know the language. He eventually made millions. Seeing my father's success created my belief system and set me on a pathway to try to reach goals like my father. My belief system was created in a file in my mind titled "Risk and Financial Success". Because of this file, I have taken many risks in business, and on occasion I have earned up to six figures of income in little over a month. The attitudes from my belief system were those of not being afraid to take a risk and thinking outside the box. The first business I started on my own was with a partner who backed out a week before we were supposed to move into an office space. I chose to move forward without him, which was a major risk. But my risk paid off; I became one of the top producers in that field.

I have not always succeeded with each risk I have taken. In fact, I have made many mistakes and suffered many losses. These losses still can cause me to pull back from risk taking. Sometimes I feel frozen in fear. This is my battle, and I choose to engage in it because I want to win it.

We all have some self-created belief systems. I am now going to share some ideas to help us create a new healthy belief system purposefully so we can create new, positive habits.

HABIT #1 *Push Through, Especially When You Want to Quit*

When you feel like quitting, stop and acknowledge what you are feeling, but don't dwell on it because that will push you to eventually quit. Instead ask yourself, "What is causing me to want to quit?" Is it your long term belief system or is it that you are trying to move beyond this point in your life and you are experiencing temporary fear? It's easy to start something but following through is where most people fail. Once you are aware of what is really driving you to want to quit, make a decision to push through until the next day. Tomorrow may bring you the result you need or the drive you need to break through.

HABIT #2 *"Check Into" Reality*

Sit down and analyze what is really going on in your life financially instead of hoping things will simply work out at the end. The truth hurts when it hasn't been acknowledged for a long time. If you find trouble in your financial life, the damage done can always be fixed. Dealing with it now is always better than dealing with it tomorrow. If you wait before taking action, you are only waiting to see more bills piling up.

HABIT #3 *Spend Your Time in Productive Activity*

"The principle [Pareto Principle, also known as the 80/20 rule] was suggested by management thinker Joseph M. Juran. It was named after the Italian economist Vilfredo Pareto, who observed that 80% of income in Italy was received by 20% of the Italian population. The assumption is that most of the results in any situation are determined by a small number of causes." ~ Wikipedia

"We find that the top 20 percent of people, natural forces, economic inputs, or any other causes we can measure typically lead to about 80% of results, outputs, or effects" ~ Richard Koch

About 20% of our financial activities account for 80% of our financial results. As I shared in the negative habits, when we check out of reality we focus on non-productive activities that produce 80% of our negative results. Remember, 80% of our financial problems come from 20% of the activities that we do. Think about what productive activities produce the most profit. Write them down and then spend most of your time doing those activities.

HABIT #4 *Investing in Yourself – Abundance Thinking*

Abundance Thinking increases our possibilities. You've heard it said where there is a will there a way. If I told you to go to a seminar in 3 days from now because it may help you financially, you could probably tell me all the excuses of why you don't have the money or the time. Yet, if I told you that I would give you $5,000 when you got there, you would most likely find a way to come up with the money and make the time to get to this seminar. What happened? When you are truly committed, you will always find a way to get what you desire. Why? Our true desire leads to intense focus on finding the solution. This is *Abundance Thinking*.

Investing in yourself helps you to make wiser and better decisions so that your efforts in other investments will have a leg up towards true success. Not only will personal growth investment help you improve your decisions, it will also improve all areas of your life.

You may think it a bit lavish, but over the past few years I have invested close to six figures in personal growth coaching, workshops, seminars, and retreats. However, the return on these investments has been priceless. I would never have reached a six figure income in a matter of months without this personal growth investment. Beyond that, by investing in personal growth I have learned much about myself, my thoughts, my motivations, my weaknesses, and my strengths, so my relationships with others has become richer, deeper, and more meaningful. Don't sell yourself short by not investing in yourself.

Habit #5 Take Personal Responsibility

The decisions we have made are what put us in the financial position we are currently in. We allow credit card companies to charge us fees by being nonchalant about paying our bills. We take responsibility for the fees, but never look to see how to avoid other unnecessary charges. In other words, we keep spending without reason since we are not aware of our financial situation. We choose victimhood if we keep paying for something because we can't control our spending. Yet we say things like: "I don't know where all my money goes!"

If we can't match up what we are making with what we are spending, we are essentially "checked out" of reality. Living like this is like a runaway train: It's only a matter of time before it crashes. Don't let a financial crash become the lightning rod to shock you into making a change. Taking personal responsibility now helps us to wake up before we hit the wall financially. When you take responsibility for the results you currently have it also gives you the power to change. You now have the ability to respond versus react to your financial situation.

Habit #6 Give 100% ~ Play to Win

Here's a new way of thinking about money: "Money is chasing me". If you choose to have faith like this, you are training your mind to attract economic success. As a man thinks, so he is. Such thinking changes the attitude with which you present yourself to the world, making you more attractive to those who can offer you genuine opportunities for growth and success. With such a mindset, you will start to see the calls and offers knocking at your door. Ask, seek, and knock, and the door will be opened. Trust that the giver on the other side is not going to give you something hurtful but beneficial. When you are convinced that the giver wants you to win, you will play your life to win versus fearing that you are going to lose. When you play to win, you will give 100% of your heart which will allow you to give all you've got in this game called life.

God's Got Your Back

Just like learning how to ride a bike or driving a manual transmission operated car, mistakes during your first attempt is inevitable. Don't be discouraged when you are starting off; don't give up and head back to your old patterns of ineffective behavior. Instead, celebrate both the victories and the failures. Understand that you have more power in you than you know. Your mind is powerful, and your heart is just as powerful. Your Creator wants you to change the cycle that keeps you from becoming the person you want to be, and ultimately, who you were designed to be.

There is much to do for God as a wise steward of the money that He gives you. God indeed wants to bless you: You may not have a high self-worth, but to God you are His priceless creation. He thinks you are worthy enough for His one and only Son to die for you. God wants you to break your self-destructive cycles more than you do. He wants your heart, mind, soul, and strength for the purpose of bringing about goodness and prosperity. When we choose to stay in our destructive patterns of irresponsibility, we are actually choosing to have the Evil One, who is by nature a deceiver and destroyer, as our protector. This is madness! Why let the fox continue to guard the hen house—especially after he has already stolen and eaten half the flock? The Evil One has run your finances for too long. But that does not satisfy him. He wants to wreck your finances now and then pass that ruin

85

onto your children and the subsequent generations of your descendents. This financial curse has been around for too long. God has your heart's desire waiting for you. It's time for you to stand up and claim what has been already yours from the beginning!

"Do not be misled: Bad company corrupts good character" –
1 Corinthians 15:33

As much as our habits contribute to where we are financially, our counselors are another reason. Have you ever hung out with someone who spoke a certain way or said a certain word all the time when they spoke? Did you find yourself repeating what they say? Like it or not, we mirror the character of those with whom we spend significant amounts of time.

The Bible warns, "Do not be misled: Bad company corrupts good character" (1 Corinthians 15:33). The reverse also is true. Good company encourages good character. The scriptures speak volumes about being careful not to adopt the ways of the wrong influences around us.

I went out to breakfast with a friend of mine who owns a multimillion dollar company so I could ask for advice and guidance on a new business decision in my life. As he spoke, every book I'd read, CD I'd listened to, seminar I'd attended, and the ups and downs I'd experienced in the financial arena were resonating in my mind. Don't get me wrong; during this lunch appointment I learned a lot of new information. However, he made the old information that I had already known seem fresh and new. Why?

Because he had lived it. Old information seems to be new when spoken with conviction from personal experience.

My friend was where I wanted to be. He was living the knowledge I sought to ingrain in my mind. Knowledge without action is wishing; knowledge with action is wisdom. This man sitting across from me had the same knowledge I had yet only one of us had a multi-million dollar company. What was the difference? One applied it and the other didn't. One had surrounded himself with specific people who were more equipped than he was to strengthen the areas where he was weak. He told me this: "Pick your advisors wisely. Get advice from the people who are where you want to be." I had to let that sink in. Then he continued, "Would you go to a divorced man to ask for marriage counseling? Would you go to a person who was overweight to help you lose weight? Would you call a plumber to fix your teeth?"

All these rhetorical questions led me to ask myself: "Why do I surround myself with advisors who cannot help me get where I want to go in life?" All too often, we hang out with people who are unable to help us grow because it's our way of staying comfortable. We are used to familiar patterns, so we find associates who fit those patterns in order to avoid an internal battle to change who we are. Look around you and you will see dead men and women walking. By this I mean that altogether too many people are defeated financially. These same people have given up and settled for little or nothing in terms of their pursuit of success. In this crowd, a comfortable acceptance of one's status quo is the norm. In this crowd, no one will challenge you financially. If they do, it will likely fall flat because of a lack of application in their own lives.

We subconsciously seek the company of those who will advise us only what we want to hear because our belief system leads us there. Remember that our belief system has fought for its own existence. The habits we created were for that very purpose. The company you keep is there as well for that very purpose. Choose your advisors wisely. Remember: The blind cannot lead the blind.

Now let us address this matter: In order to change the company we keep we may indeed lose some of the friends whom we currently hold dear. I know that sounds cruel, but what I am suggesting is that you ought not to keep toxic relationships that do not promote you out of your comfort zone. You may offend some of your running buddies by deciding to seek the counsel of financially wise people. People don't want to feel left out. They will either follow you or pull you back. Most people blame their misfortune on the rich. Resentment is soon to follow and no one wants to hang out with people you resent.

Renowned author Robert Kiyosaki, of *Rich Dad, Poor Dad* fame, said his rich dad was surrounded by people who worked for him but none of them would take the risk to sit down and ask for advice on how to get where he was. I see that happening every day. I saw that happening in my own life. I have been in the company of people who are very wise financially but my ego and fear of being judged caused me to stand in silence rather than seeking their advice. I ultimately had to push myself to act upon my thinking to enter the discomfort zone of seeking wise financial counsel.

Time Is Money

How you spend your time is a great indicator of where your dollars are going. Waste time being idle and you will find yourself wasting money in the same way. We've all heard the old saying, "Birds of a feather flock together." This is exceptionally true of idle people: They choose to hang out with others who are also engaged in doing nothing at all. On the other hand, productive people value time and refuse to waste it. I'm not saying that such people don't have leisure time to relax. What I am saying is that productive people plan out their time, including how they spend their leisure hours.

We are always creating a space around us made up of who we are. We do this by actively inviting or passively permitting those whom we want to imitate into our lives. Like it or not, we attract what we subconsciously want the most in our lives. My friend told me once that he has two executives to whom he reports. If he needs something important to get done at the executive level, my friend approaches the executive who is busy instead of the one who is idle. Isn't this counterintuitive? At first glance, yes. However, my friend has learned something important about human character: Busy people get things done because they are busy!

Success will only come to us if we choose to control our use of time and actively prevent idle distractions from pulling us away from important activities. Socializing with friends is enjoyable and therapeutic, but if it occurs during your peak work hours the joy we get from it will turn to misery when we see how grievously it disrupts our productivity. Does this mean that we need to stay busy and work hard during every waking moment? No, but take my friend's advice: "When I work, I work, and I don't have play time. When I get home, I am home, and work stops." In other words, give yourself to work when you need to work, and bank your time for leisure so that it will not impact your productivity. Trouble always follows when we mix work time and leisure time.

PRIDE and GREED: Killers of Financial Freedom

Pride: the quality or state of being proud. Inordinate self-esteem; conceit.

There are two character flaws I have encountered which more than anything else keep us from achieving our financial goals: pride and greed.

I have seen people walk away from making millions because of pride and reed. Pride is being concerned more with a title or a position than producing revenue. Pride says, "Look at me, I am somebody." Pride makes the beggar feel like the chooser. Pride makes us forget where we come from, where we currently are, and where we're really going. I have seen people go broke all the while clinging desperately to their pride.

Greed, which is a sibling in sin to pride, is the second most common character flaw which holds us back from achieving wealth. How then shall we define Greed? It is wanting excessively more than you already have or focusing on *getting* to the exclusion of *giving*. Greed is like starving man who wolfs down the first available food. It is activated by our survival instincts, causing us to glut ourselves for self-preservation and turning our attention away from giving to others. I have fasted purposely for multiple days at a time. During one particular fast I limited myself to liquid only for seven days. After the fast, I went out and celebrated my self-control by overindulging in a big meal. Guess what happened? My body rejected the food and I threw up. My stomach had shrunk and my body needed to be fed gradually until it could expand back to its normal size.

Greed is a response to financial starvation. When struggling people see the opportunity to make more money they go after it like they've never seen money before. Unfortunately, they will likely chase the money away. Their stomachs are no fuller than when they started their meal. They, in a sense, "throw up" the money they accumulated. If they don't throw it up, they will spend it as fast as they earn it. When people are not used to having money their dysfunction belief system kicks in gear and they begin buying material possessions as an overreaction to previous times of want in their past. They will start buying stuff just because they have the money, not because it's a need. Such behavior ultimately leaves people in need. Buyer beware: these two deadly flaws, pride and greed, reside in each of us and they are awakened most easily by money.

Let's take a look at how pride and greed show up in our personalities when dealing with money:

- *"The Miser"* or the Taker: This is the person who wants to get paid and doesn't care if anyone else makes a dime or not.

- *"The Martyr"* or the Rescuer: This is the person who wants to earn money in order to help others. Such people are happy to make others successful, yet they are a victim to everyone else that wins. They allow people to walk all over them and wonder why they're broke.

- *"The Meddler"* or the Abuser: This is the person who can't get ahead financially who then projects his failure on others and blocks them from getting ahead as well. If this person can't win, then they make sure that others can't win either. Misery loves company.

In order to have a "win-win" situation, we need to embrace a personality that is the opposite of the above. This personality will master all others. "The Master" or the Producer: This is the person who has the proper mind and heart regarding money. This person indeed pursues success for his own benefit but he then shares his success through teaching others the wisdom of how he got there. This is the truly generous person.

It's Just a Late Fee!

Who takes the time to think about late fees? Only those who have the discipline to watch their balances so that they don't have to pay late fees!

Here are some facts about late fees in the U.S.:

- US Bank stands to collect a record of $38.5 billion in fees for customer overdrafts in the year 2010.

- Penalty fees from credit cards added up to about $20.5 billion in 2009, according to R.K. Hammer, a consultant to the credit card industry. (Source: New York Times, September 2009.)

- Between 2008 and 2009, 15 % of American adults, or nearly 34 million people, have been late making a credit card payment and 8 percent (18 million people) have missed a payment entirely.(Source: National Foundation for credit counseling, 2009 Financial Literacy Survey, April 2009)

- 26% of Americans, or more than 58 million adults, admit to not paying all of their bills on time. *(Source: National Foundation for credit counseling)*

Have you ever asked yourself, "Why am I paying late fees?" The answer is related to your character. You need to be able to manage both your money and your time to be able to prevent paying late fees. The next question to ask is: "I realize that I will pay unnecessary fees if I'm late on this bill. Why am I late in the first place?" Oftentimes, people answer this question by shifting blame, making scapegoats of the economy, their income level (or lack thereof), or their overall financial problems. Nevertheless, no matter what the outward circumstances, there is always an inward reason for the late fee problem. That reason is our conscious or subconscious choice to "check out" of reality when the bill arrives. Whether we're struggling to make ends meet, to grow, to change, or to improve financially, we can easily shut down emotionally.

In such situations where our emotions have taken over, the logic of paying a bill on time and avoiding a late fee doesn't make much sense. "The lights are on, but nobody's home" is a saying that would fit the description of someone who "checks out" of reality financially. It's unfortunate that the very people who pay most of the late fees are the people who struggle with living paycheck to paycheck. Most people don't think twice in paying late fees. Some actually get used to it some much so, that it's subconsciously added to their budgets, even if they don't formally have one.

One time I got smart and switched monthly billing expenses from an online video rental company which cost me $19 per month for unlimited movie rentals to a company that would charge me $1 per rental for the same type of service. In my mind it made total sense to switch because I generally rented only 4 movies a month, thus I would be saving $15 month. After I switched, I did start seeing the savings, so I applauded myself for making a wise choice.

My applause was quickly muted, however, when I received my monthly bank statement. I noticed that I got charged 3 times, at $33 per event, in overdraft fees related to my $1 DVD rentals. Because I wasn't paying close to my attention to my finances, I paid $99 in overdraft fees for $3 in movie rentals. I should have allowed this unnecessary cost teach me a lesson, but I didn't let it sink in deep enough and I let it happen to me again sometime later. All in all, I went from saving $15 a month to spending $198 on over draft fees!

I share the blame with so many other people who will contribute to our national financial waste by paying $38 billion in overdraft fees on our credit cards, mortgages, bounced checks, and the like. The first time I paid that ridiculous overdraft charge I was bothered, but I was not bothered enough to correct the problem...instead I "checked out" of reality. I allowed myself to waste more money again through another overdraft not too long thereafter. When I am "checked out" of reality, paying unnecessary fees doesn't feel as painful as it should.

Here is a great quote that captures my point: *"A shocking occurrence ceases to be shocking when it occurs daily." – Alexander Chase*

Financial Coma

"A little extra sleep, a little more slumber, a little folding of the hands to rest- then poverty will pounce on you like a bandit; scarcity will attack you like an armed robber."
Proverbs 24: 33-34 (NLT)

Financial pressure causes many people to "check out" emotionally, and fall into a financial coma. The banks, credit card companies, and utilities companies love these financial deep sleepers because of the billions they generate yearly for absolutely no product or service. Nothing of real consequence happens overnight, rather by a series of choices. The scripture above says that merely a "little" sleep will result in poverty. It didn't say a lot of sleep. It's the series of little choices that we make in "checking out" of reality here and there which can seem harmless but in the end leads to a violent break-in by poverty. Poverty doesn't sneak up on us when we are awake but only when we are asleep.

The scripture describes a "checked-out" mind as a thief. Why? Just like a thief, a checked-out mind (which revels in its sleepy state) actually steals our productivity and results in poverty. Poverty is a state of mind, a habit which comes to us when we check out of reality and go into sleep mode. Be alert...Be self controlled and...Stay awake!

"Do not love sleep or you will grow poor; stay awake and you will have food to spare." Proverbs 20:13

Here are 3 action steps to counteract the financial sleep mode:

1. Be Alert

We sense danger when we are alert. On the other hand, we can't sense danger when we are sound asleep. A state of awareness is a state of being alert or being awake. When we're awake, we can see the robber trying to break into our bank accounts. Balancing your checkbook, financial planning for the future, identifying your belief system, and figuring out where all your money goes, are all means to help us to stay in reality and can become habits if practiced consistently. Checking out of reality is also a habit. We must replace this habit by applying new habits as I mentioned above.

"The prudent see danger and take refuge, but the simple keep going and suffer for it" Proverbs 27:12 (NIV)

2. Be Self Controlled

Self-control is no easy feat. It's easy to control material stuff but controlling oneself is an entirely different matter. A shopping spree when you are broke is a lack of self control. Financing our purchases with credit is a lack of self control. Paying unnecessary late fees is a lack of self control.

Money can be controlled by a self-controlled person. Money does not have any control in itself. Money is nothing more than paper which is backed up by a commonly perceived value. We cannot control the value of the dollar but we can control what we do with it.

3. Stay Awake

Don't allow circumstances to lull you to sleep. Surround yourself with people who can hold you accountable. Sometimes, it's hard to see what you're doing until you have to pay the fees. Usually, it is too late. Go over this chapter from time to time to refresh your memory of the new information you just learned. We forget 80% of what we hear and read so it's important to remind yourself with repetition. Repetition is the mother of all learning and produces habits. Therefore, consistently apply what you learn to your life and you will make it stick. *Knowledge without action is wishing. Knowledge with action is wisdom.*

Chapter 4

HEALTH AWARENESS

Health Starts With a Healthy Mind

When I was growing up my father had several heart attacks. I never understood why his doctor had him switch what he ate to healthier food. I remember tasting the "healthy" food and it didn't seem like it had much flavor. I also remember that my father ate very unhealthy foods disregarding what the doctor advised. He ended up having diabetes and later on in life he eventually died of a stroke. As I grew up I had this constant fear of having diabetes. I had no knowledge of the disease. I believed that I would automatically have diabetes since it runs in my family. This belief was constantly in my head even though I tried not to think about it.

One day I had a conversation with one of my very close friends who is knowledgeable about health. My friend told me that the decisions I make regarding my health will determine the fate of my health. That day my mindset changed. I began a journey to break the myths that I believed about being healthy and unhealthy. I started to acquire knowledge about diabetes and how it generates. The more I became aware of the new knowledge, the more I became hopeful about being healthy. In other words, I gained faith and belief that it was up to me to create a healthy lifestyle. As a result, I started to make better choices about my health. As I applied my new knowledge, I started to see results almost immediately. I went from being 185lbs to 145lbs in less than a year, and went from being sick what seemed like every other month to not having the flu or colds for over 8 years.

As I continued on my journey to keep a healthy lifestyle, I noticed the choice of foods I selected came from a belief. I realized, as with every other area mentioned in this book, there is always a root to every problem and until you deal with the root, the unwanted results keep showing up.

Food = Joy

After taking several classes on how my belief systems affected everything I do in my life, I started to see that my choices of being unhealthy were not just random choices. I seemed to always have this justification after I made the wrong choice of food; I felt like I deserved it. I started to think of what subconscious program ran this type of thinking. I remember watching my father eating for comfort and my mother drinking her problems away. These examples began to program my "Health" file with the belief "food will make me feel different".

Russell Friedman and John James, founders of *Grief Recovery Institute*, said that the way we deal with our grief is directly impacted by what we saw or what we were told regarding our grief growing up. Friedman and James talk about Short Term Energy Relief Behaviors (STERBs) being anything we use to change how we feel. The list of STERBs goes beyond just food or drinking it can be anything you use to distract you from what you are actually feeling.

Friedman and James named a few other STERBs like alcohol or drugs, exercise, sex, fantasy (movies, TV, books, computer), isolation, shopping (also called retail therapy). Food is one of the most common and most socially accepted STERBs. Think about it. You don't get arrested for overeating food, but you will for over-drinking alcohol.

Looking back at my father and mother, they were both STERBing while they were grieving so it made total sense to me why I would turn to food and drinking when I grieved. Whenever I felt down emotionally, I wanted to eat something. The craving didn't actually come from hunger but from the attempt to fulfill the emptiness brought by my grief. The more I tried to satisfy that emptiness the more I ate to bring my body back to a state of happiness. This was only a temporary fix. Everyone has a different way of dealing with their pain. For some it's food for others it's drugs, or any of the STERBs listed above. People go to these to bring back their happy state of mind from the imbalance caused by their grief.

As soon as my body felt the grief, it began to search my mind for the file which brought me happiness. Since my mind was programmed with happy thoughts which were connected to food, food then became a fix just like a drug. Sometimes the mind will go to a specific type of food to fill the craving. For example, I started to notice that every time I was feeling down about something, I would crave ice cream. I remember going to get a specific type of ice cream, a "Drumstick". I never understood why until I remembered having one of the most joyful times growing up. It was when my family and I went to the movies and had ice cream during the intermission. Back in those days there was always a commercial for an ice cream break in the middle of the movie. Can you guess what type of ice cream was advertised? You guessed it: "Drumstick".

I still remember the music and I still see myself running around the theater jumping with joy. This was a very joyful time not only because of the ice cream but because my family was together and happy. My mind programmed this memory with food and happiness. As I mentioned before, my mind naturally searched for my source of happiness (ice cream) in the attempt to bring back happiness even has an adult. Once I became aware of my automatic subconscious choice, I started to make more a conscious choice. I realized that ice cream equaled joy and happiness. It was my fix. I also chose drinking alcohol as another way to deal with my grief. For me alcohol represented power and courage. When my mother was drinking, she seemed to have more power and courage to stand up to my dad.

I have met many people who came to realize that food was rooted to the feeling of being accepted and loved. Once I met a man who took one of my workshops, he was dumfounded by the revelation that he attached food with love. When he was a kid, dinner time was one of the only times when he felt like his family loved each other. They would talk with each other and be happy at dinner time. The rest of the time outside of "dinner" was a living nightmare. These memories were imprinted in his mind under a file named "Food Equals Love". He naturally attached food to love. He ended up being overweight and almost died of several heart conditions due to his unhealthy eating habits.

Unfortunately, this belief system took the life of his sister who could not give up overeating. She was massively overweight and eventually ate herself to death. When she was asked to cut down her eating habits, her belief systems translated that people were asking her to stop feeling loved. Giving up overeating was like asking her to cut her arm off. Food became an addiction. With any addiction, when left untreated, the end result is self-destruction. Think about the choice you make regarding food. Are these choices getting you closer to your health goals, or are they getting you closer to self-destruction? I know food is not the only thing which can cause us to become unhealthy. Yet, a lot of times it starts with food and can lead to abuse of other substances like drugs and alcohol. Again, it's not about the substance but what the substance represents to you.

Another example I saw of a substance representing much more than itself was through a gentleman I met who said he struggled with drinking alcohol. He realized that the main reason he craved the alcohol was connected to a memory of his Dad and him drinking together. He recalls those times being the only time they were able to talk and enjoy each other. His father was never there for him emotionally, yet when it came to drinking he seemed to always have time. Drinking became a source of happiness and connection for my friend. His belief system was that you must drink in order to connect and have fun. Of course, the opposite results showed up but his mind kept going back to the same belief. Your situation might not be as dramatic as these examples.

If you have a hard time quitting something, or anything which doesn't help you to be healthy, then you may want to ask yourself what it really represents to you.

What You Think of Yourself Directly Impacts How You Deal With Your Health

"Eighty-seven to 95 percent of the illnesses that plague us today are a direct result of our thought life. What we think about affects us physically and emotionally. It's an epidemic of toxic emotions." ~ Cognitive Neuroscientist, Dr. Caroline Leaf

Think about what you are saying to yourself when you feel sad, discouraged, fearful, or any other negative emotion. Your negative emotions are usually directly connected to the negative label you give yourself. I noticed that the times I went for ice cream was when I felt rejected and labeled myself as not worthy, or stupid, or hopeless. After I had my ice cream fix, and the sugar high dropped, my feelings always matched what I labeled myself before eating the ice cream. I felt worthless and unhappy, which was the very feeling I tried to avoid. The way you think about yourself will affect how you label yourself. This will affect the way you feel, and ultimately will direct the choices you make about your health.

When you are feeling bad about yourself, you tend to crave things that "look" helpful or like they will cheer you up, but in the end make you feel the way you actually labeled yourself. This is a self-fulfilling prophecy. When it comes to health, the label you give in your mind will show up on the outside. Some people who think they are fat and undesirable tend to communicate that by what they eat. The end result is they become overweight. Once they reach being overweight then the negative self-worth label matches. On the other hand, if they think they are fat when they are not the prophecy still works the same. The result is that they see themselves on the outside as fat. The label will still fit regardless of what anyone else says to them. The same thing goes for drinking, smoking or using drugs. The end result, or price the person is paying for these bad habits, will always match their true self-worth.

A good indicator of the label you give yourself is the way you feel after giving in to your craving. When you have a good label of yourself the choices of food will have to match your label. A lot of people think and say they are making healthy choices but their results show the opposite. They say things like "I feel like I am healthy", yet their actions show otherwise. The true feeling of being healthy only comes after taking action to be healthy. I am not saying all unhealthy people have a low self-esteem. Many doctors and studies have shown that a low self-worth won't lead you to make good healthy choices, and a high self-worth increases your chance of making healthy choices. *"A large study by MacArthur Foundation found that high self-esteem is a powerful predictor of health and longevity. If you don't feel good about yourself today, you likely will not fare as well as someone who has high self-worth and a positive attitude." Lifelong Health by Dr. David Lipschitz*

The Security Gate to Your Health

We have all been to the airport where we have to go through a security gate to make sure there are no dangerous objects which will threat public safety. The need for security has increased a lot more since September 11, 2001 (9/11). The bigger the threat, the tighter the security becomes. Our mind is like a guard at the airport security gate. It defines every item as safe or not safe. The items in this case are the foods we eat, the liquids we drink, or whatever else we allow inside our bodies. Once the security guard of our mind allows the items to go through even if they are unsafe, they will become "safe". No matter what anybody says, these items will go through even if the warning lights are going off. Just like my example of the woman who died of over eating, the mind of a person with low self-worth will allow dangers through the security gate even if it kills them.

There are only three common actions we do daily that allow these items to enter our body which directly affects our health. These actions are breathing, drinking, and eating. What we breathe, drink, and eat are the natural ways our bodies take what is on the outside to the inside. These actions will result in life or death. A great habit to develop is to ask questions before you do these actions. Ask yourself if what you're about to inhale will bring life or death to your health. When drinking, ask yourself if the liquids (and/or the amount you are drinking) will bring more life or death to your health. The same goes with what you are eating. Ask yourself if this food will bring life or death to your body.

Most people won't ask these questions because of excuses, justifications, and rationalizations. Nevertheless, it doesn't stop their health from moving towards death or life. The main reason people will keep doing things at the expense of their health is because it doesn't kill them right away. They can still appear ok on the outside, but taking in the unhealthy items over a period of time adds up to big problems later. Nothing happens overnight.

Here are 5 action steps you can take to make sure you bring life versus death to your health:

#1 Check the Items

As I mentioned earlier, when we feel a threat we increase protection to ourselves and our material possessions by installing an alarm system, hiring security guards, and increasing law enforcement. We spend money, time and energy to protect us from the outside world. The interesting thing is that we can be more concerned about protecting our stuff than watching what goes into our bodies.

Most of us leave the gate wide open to the food we eat. We invite almost everything to come inside our system without checking the items. There is an attack everyday on our health and we are not even aware of it. The reason we are not alarmed or aware is because we do not feel a threat anymore. What used to be a threat becomes an ally.

As I mentioned before the root is usually attached to our self-worth. When you don't have a high value for your self-worth, you won't take good care of your health. You won't make the time to take care of yourself. You won't take the time to check the items that goes through your security system. In a way, we are subconsciously punishing ourselves by not taking care of our health in order to fit the low self-worth label.

Our body has a natural ability to get used to what items we call "safe". Your natural balance, or homeostasis, will adjust and actually start to like and crave unhealthy foods and reject healthy foods. Yet when you change your unhealthy habits to healthy habits, the body at first will resist but then it will eventually accept it and adjust to the new items (foods, drinks, etc.). Your body will start to reject the unhealthy foods when you keep feeding it healthy foods.

I recall when I first gave up eating unhealthy foods I had an opportunity to eat some junk food. I wolfed it down only to throw up right after I ate it. My body was finally recognizing the healthy items and rejecting   the   unhealthy   items.

#2 *Fire Your Security Guard*

After 9/11 the government replaced all the airport security guard companies. They fired the old security guards and replaced them with new ones. The same can be done with the security guard of our mind. The things our mind counts right now as "safe" when they are actually "unsafe" need to be redefined.

I remember when I was a teen working at a bank as a security guard and the bank got robbed 5 times in 6 months. Apparently the robbers knew that I was inexperienced and oblivious, because it all happened under my nose. Sometimes I saw them as they walked in the door of the bank, but other times I didn't notice them walking through the door at all. I have a feeling that these robbers probably studied me out and knew they could get away with it. The security guard company sent another security guard who was much more alert than I was and the robberies stopped. It took getting another security guard to stop the problem.

The security guard of your mind is your mindset about health. You need to fire the mindset that keeps bringing unhealthy choices of food and change to a healthy mindset that will bring better choices. The new mindset and label can only come from the decision to educate yourself with new applied knowledge.

When I started to read books like *Fast Food Nation* by Eric Schlosser and watching different documentaries like *Super Size Me* by Morgan Spurlock, I started to be aware of the consequences of the choices I was making. I was reprogramming my mind to reject the unhealthy habits. It's not only good to increase your knowledge you must also apply the new knowledge.

The choices that you make to change your health you will in turn start to build your self-worth. The more healthy choices you make the better you feel about you. Once your self-worth is built, the security guard of your mind regarding the items you allow to enter your body will be built up as well. Yet nothing will happen overnight. I would suggest that you start cutting back on the unhealthy habits little by little every day. If you move to fast you could send you body to shock and it will rebel against you.

#3 Be Aware Of The Disguise

The mind gets very tricky when you attempt to make any changes, especially if it's something you have been doing for a long time. Going back to the analogy of the items going through a security check point at the airport, the terrorists who are trying to come through that gate are not going to dress up like terrorists. They are going to wear something which will not attract much attention to themselves.

In the same way, the mind will try to disguise the items by justifying and reasoning within your head that they are safe. It will tell you things like "you deserve this", "it's a harmless piece of chocolate cake", "you offend people by eating healthy", or "I don't have the time to eat healthy". The security guard of your mind will either convince you that everything is okay or flat out deny that you have a problem.

Once you give into the first temptation, another convincing conversation usually seems follow soon after. Then the habits of allowing the unwanted or unsafe items are now reprogrammed in your mind as safe items again. Now you are looking at your waistline and wondering how in the world it grew so fast. But this time it's not alarming since your mind and body are now used to this item being safe. These items tend to be what I call a punishment disguised as a reward. Think about it, you are trying to eat healthy and you've been working really hard and then you go for something off your health plan a few times. "No big deal", you think to yourself. Yet the craving for more seems to come back with a vengeance and the next thing you know it's back to the usual amount.

Another mind trick is the subconscious thinking that our metabolism won't change as we get older. I used to hear people say that the older you get slower the metabolism works. I didn't think it applied to me. When I was young I could eat anything and it would take a long time to get to my waistline. I had a very high metabolism. My ego had a hard time adjusting. It seemed like the older I got, my body became less forgiving of my mistakes. The truth is the older we get, the tougher our security guard should be.

#4 Pay Attention to Your Comfort Zone

The dictionary definition of the word convenience is the quality of being suitable to one's comfort, purposes, or needs. We live in a fast paced world. We want everything yesterday. Everyone around us,

114

including ourselves, is busy so we have to eat on the run. We drive to the nearest fast food place we see. It's called "fast" food because it's fast which makes it convenient. The truth is we usually give in to what is convenient and comfortable for us in the short term. Most people go with the flow with what's socially acceptable. If you try to change the flow of what most people do, you will have resistance. You'll be going against the current.

I have many times failed to hold on to the convictions that I have on eating healthy because it's much easier and faster to go with the flow. In other words, it is more convenient. The reason we strive for convenience is so we can be more comfortable. To comfort means to soothe in time of affliction or distress. The root is also stress or affliction which is a form of grief. We tend to avoid dealing with our grief by seeking to soothe our affliction with convenient and/or comfort foods. We seek convenience even with the people around us. We don't like to rock the boat.

As I wrote earlier, you eventually become like the people you surround yourself with. If you are going to be healthy, understand that it will be inconvenient. It will not go with the flow with what's going on around you. You may be at a party where everyone is making unhealthy choices, but you must stand in your conviction of being healthy. The problem with convenience is that you don't feel like you're paying the price now, however you will pay for it later.

In the book *The Slight Edge*, Jeff Olson writes, "The people living on top, who take responsibility, live a life that is in some ways uncomfortable. Successful people do what unsuccessful people are not willing to do, and that often means living outside the limits of one's comfort zone. When you're one out of twenty, you're always going to be going in the opposite direction from the other nineteen." And he goes on to say, "What's uncomfortable early becomes comfortable later...What's comfortable early becomes uncomfortable later."

#5 *Get Your Support In Place*

I remember when I started eating healthy the word organic was not a popular term. Every time I used the term people thought I was a "weirdo". I received much persecution from my friends and family who were thinking I was going to die because I didn't eat "regular" foods. I was ridiculed and talked about behind my back, but I did not quit even though it was uncomfortable and inconvenient. I didn't give in at parties; I probably offended people by not eating what was offered.

Some, with good intention, will attempt to stop you. They may give you warnings and tell you what you are doing is too extreme, or give you all the reasons why it will hurt you. Most people will want to pull you back because they don't like to be exposed.

When you focus on being healthy you now become a light shining on the area they fall short. However, most of your resistance will come from yourself. When you focus on overcoming your own inner battle, the outer battles will be easier to overcome. As you start being healthy you will attract other people who also want to become healthy.

Now I see the word organic being the "cool" thing. Even fast food restaurants advertise healthy food. My friends now are all into "healthy" eating. They now respect my conviction about eating healthy foods. One of my favorite quotes that captures this point is "All truth passes through three stages. First, it is ridiculed. Second, it is violently opposed. Third, it is accepted as being self-evident."~Arthur Schopenhauer

A great friend of mine became my accountability partner. We made a deal that anytime either of us ate outside of our commitment to eat healthy, we would have to call the other person and tell them about it. After several calls to my friend confessing my short falls, I began to muster a stronger conviction to say no to unhealthy food. An accountability partner or group is essential to keep you on the path of being healthy. When picking your accountability partner make sure you pick one who has as much or more conviction as you do about being healthy. As the saying goes, "Pity the man who falls and has no one to help him." Two is better than one.

Next Generation Health

Now that you have a checkpoint to get your health in a different direction, let's take a look at some facts about the health condition of the United States. As I mentioned before when our mind makes something unsafe safe, we lose a sense of reality. We lose touch with the facts about the unhealthy foods we eat and what it really does to our health.

Obesity is common, serious and costly:

- More than one-third of U.S. adults (35.7%) are obese

- No state has met the nation's Healthy People 2010 goal to lower obesity prevalence to 15%

- The number of states with an obesity prevalence of 30% or more has increased to 12 states in 2010

- In 2009, nine states had obesity rates of 30% or more

- In 2000, no state had an obesity prevalence of 30% or more

- Obesity-related conditions include heart disease, stroke, type 2 diabetes and certain types of cancer, some of the leading causes of death

- In 2008, medical costs associated with obesity were estimated at $147 billion; the medical costs paid by third-party payors for people who are obese were $1,429 higher than those of normal weight [4]

One of the costs of eating unhealthy is obesity. Obesity is now considered a disease by some experts. One of the many arguments I had while I was eating healthy was the fact that the generation that came before us did not die or have health problems from eating the same food we are eating now. I would get this statement, "My parents never had a problem with their health and they eat like I do." It may true that your parents might have been healthier than you, but they didn't eat the way we do. Not only the amount that we eat has radically changed, but also there's been a change to the quality of the food we eat. Based on the statistic above, I believe this change has not been for the better. Here's another article which drives my point home:

"The obesity epidemic arrived with astonishing speed. After tens of thousands

[4] Source: **http://www.cdc.gov/obesity/data/adult.html**

of generations of human evolution, flab has become widespread only in the past 50 years, and waistlines have ballooned exponentially in the last two decades. In 1980, 46 percent of U.S. Adults were overweight: by 2000, the figure was 64.5 percent: nearly a 1 percent annual increase in the ranks of the fat. At this rate, by 2040, 100 percent of American adults will be overweight and 'it may happen more quickly'", says John Foreyt of Baylor College of Medicine.[5]

Did you read that last part? At the rate of only 1 percent increase per year, 100 percent of Americans will be overweight by 2040. Like I mentioned before, nothing happens overnight. It's the daily small choices we make over time that adds up to the big changes to our health years down the line. This may seem extreme to you, but eating healthy is not a matter of being extreme or not. It's a matter of how much you want to enjoy your health while you walk on this planet. Why do people call you "too extreme" when you are health conscious and watching what you eat? People do this because what was natural and normal became unnatural and abnormal. We are now used to unnatural foods. Like I mentioned before, the security gate of your mind starts to call the unsafe food "safe".

One of my friend's kids was being teased at school for bringing his lunch which contained fruits and vegetables.

Source: www.//http: harvardmagazine.com

He became the laughing stock of his friends. I have also encountered the same ridicule with my adult friends as well. Think about this, the way people eat is so different than the old days when having a healthy meal was normal. Now being healthy could result in being mocked. Food did not go faster; instead we created "Fast Food" to fit our fast lifestyle. Our society has accepted this fast paced lifestyle as normal even though we are more stressed and unhealthy than ever before in our history. You may argue that we live longer than before. This may be true, but we live longer with the misery of being unhealthy which is not really living. It seems to me that we are dead men and women walking, but not really living. The next generation is learning to live this same kind of stressful lifestyle and adopting the same unhealthy eating habits.

Be The Change!

"Childhood obesity, also once rare, has mushroomed: 15 percent of children between ages six and 19 are now overweight, and even 10 percent of those between two and five. This may be the first generation of children who will die before their parents,"
~ John Foreyt

The first step to change is awareness that a problem exists. As you can see, there is an astounding decline in the health of our children. We are facing a serious problem. When you feel that you are "all good" then there is no need for additional information, learning, or changes. I can't help you if this is not important to you after reading this far. You need to search for the truth not just what is socially acceptable regarding health. Knowledge of the truth will create a big awareness. The truth will set you free from the slavery of your unhealthy habits. Yet the truth does not set you free by just knowing it. The freedom will come from applying the knowledge to your life. As you acquire and apply this new knowledge, you will establish a new security guard for your mind and you will be opening yourself up to a new world of health.

You may be thinking that it's too hard or too much hassle to change your health habits. Life will be too hard and a hassle if you DON'T change. It is much harder to live with heart disease, stroke, type 2 diabetes and certain types of cancer which are caused by obesity. Just saying No to unhealthy choices may not be enough when everyone you love is saying yes. It will get easier to say no the more often you make healthy choices and see the positive results in your life.

You may be asking yourself is it really worth it to put all this effort to change your health? Here is a story with you that might help answer this question:

"I awoke early, as I often did, just before sunrise to walk by the ocean's edge and greet the new day. As I moved through the misty dawn, I focused on a faint, far away motion. I saw a youth, bending and reaching and flailing arms, dancing on the beach, no doubt in celebration of the perfect day soon to begin.

As I approached, I sadly realized that the youth was not dancing to the bay, but rather bending to sift through the debris left by the night's tide, stopping now and then to pick up a starfish and then standing, to heave it back into the sea. I asked the youth the purpose of the effort. 'The tide has washed the starfish onto the beach and they cannot return to the sea by themselves', the youth replied. 'When the sun rises, they will die, unless I throw them back to the sea.'

As the youth explained, I surveyed the vast expanse of beach, stretching in both directions beyond my sight. Starfish littered the shore in numbers beyond calculation. The hopelessness of the youth's plan became clear to me and I countered, 'But there are more starfish on this beach than you can ever save before the sun is up. Surely you cannot expect to make a difference.' The youth paused briefly to consider my words, bent to pick up a starfish and threw it as far as possible. Turning to me he simply said, 'I made a difference to that one.' I left the boy and went home, deep in thought of what the boy had said. I returned to the beach and spent the rest of the day helping the boy throw starfish in to the sea." *(Based on the story "The Star Thrower" by Loren Eiseley)*

You can make a difference by being an example to others even if it impacts just one person, and even if the only person is you. If you have kids, it will matter to them and eventually to their kids. Even though there are thousands upon thousands who don't take the time to be healthier, you can be the one to make a difference. The next generation is more valuable than a starfish and it's worth it for them to understand the truth about their health. It is worth it to enjoy this life on earth and not go with the flow of everybody else. My parents had an opportunity to set an example to their children on being healthy, but they only left me an example of how to be unhealthy. I don't blame them because they might not have known any better. But regardless of the example that was set before me, I can stop the generational curse of health-related disease in my family by making a difference with what I do with my health.

You also have the power to stop the curse of whatever unhealthy habits that have been running in your family. It all starts with our daily choices that will make a massive difference over the years. All it takes is one starfish.

Are you going to be the one to make the changes necessary to impact generations after you? If not you, then who? If not now, then when? I implore you to join me in making a difference in this area of your life.

Chapter 5

SPIRITUAL AWARENESS

Spiritual: related or joined in spirit. Of, relating to supernatural beings or phenomena

Spirituality: the Quality or state of being spiritual. ~ Webster's Dictionary

My First Experience With Spirituality

I grew up in a small town in the Congo, central Africa called "Pointe-Noire" which means black dot in French. My father came from the US and settled down in Africa to start a business. He was very successful, and then he met my mother and they had 5 children. My very first experience of anything to do with spirituality came from my mother who was a Christian. As a child, I never really liked going to church because it seemed very boring. My mother, whom I respected, always wrote down her thoughts in her journal and read her bible every day. It always left me wondering why anyone would devote their morning to read, write and pray daily.

My home life was filled with turbulence. I saw my mother deal with a lot of pain. The arguments between my parents grew worse every year, but no matter what was going on or how dysfunctional life was, I always remember the devotion my mother had to reading her bible, praying, and journaling. This was a great example of how to be devoted spiritually, but I didn't get serious about my spiritual life until I was 21 years old.

Another thing that always impressed me about my mother was her love and how much she sacrificed for our family. She is, and always will be, a special part of my heart. I lived in Africa with my family until age 12, then came to the US with my dad and siblings and went to school. My mother, who was still living in Africa, passed away a year after we moved which sent me to the dark side. I didn't take this loss very well, partly because I was not there and never got the chance to say goodbye. I felt like the only person whom I felt truly loved by was gone. I did not see a reason to be a good boy anymore.

After my mother's death, my life's direction changed for the worst from age 13 through 21. I lived with an idea of what spirituality was but never knowing its true power in my life. I felt like a ship lost at sea. By the time I was 21 years old I had lived a reckless life. On the outside I was a great bachelor. I had a lot of friends, new car and my own pad. Yet on the inside I felt an empty abyss in my heart. When I was alone and didn't have to put on a happy face, the emptiness inside of me felt very deep and it seemed to be growing every night. I desperately tried filling it with women, drugs, money, and material things, but nothing could fill this emptiness. I did not want anything to do with "religion". My concept of spirituality was non-existent. Like a chameleon, I went along with what the different types of crowds around me were doing. I would hang out with whoever would accept me. I was not afraid to die. I had no clue what it meant to be spiritual.

What does it mean to be spiritual and what is spiritual in the first place? Based on the definition above *(relating to supernatural beings or phenomena), spirituality* is not of this physical world, but beyond what our conscious mind understands.

If you ask 100 people what it means to be spiritual, you will probably get 100 different answers. Your own personal definition of what spirituality means in your life will create your spiritual belief system, which will direct the values by which you operate your life. It will directly or indirectly impact your understanding of God or whatever you consider to be a "supernatural being". Your spiritual belief system will override any new definition of spirituality. In other words no matter what anyone says to you, unless your spiritual belief system agrees with it then it will reject it. Anyone who tries to change that belief system will be preaching to a stone wall.

Studies have shown that most of our programming and belief systems were set in place between the ages of 0-18 years old. As mentioned throughout this book, our programming or belief systems created a mental and emotional file called "spirituality". The word "God" triggers a lot of emotions. These emotions are attached to a past experience that created a belief system about that word. Most people connect the word "God" when speaking of spiritual things. As the dictionary says, "relating to supernatural being", I will use the name "God" as I refer to that Supernatural being. So let's start with the definition of God.

Who is God to You?

*God: the Being perfect in power, wisdom, and goodness
whom men worship as creator and ruler of the universe. ~
Webster's Dictionary*

Most people have their own definition of God, but
what I have noticed in my life and the lives of countless
others is that our description of God is usually connected
to that of our parents or another authority figure in our
childhood. God is regarded as an authority figure by many
people, and like the definition above as "a ruler of the
universe". Most of our views on spirituality and God
began long before we were involved in church or any type
of spiritual groups. As I mentioned before, we've had 50%
of our programming set in place by the time we were five
years old. Now our programming is running
subconsciously confirming our spiritual belief system just
like a self-fulfilling prophecy, making what we believe into
a reality. Blaming some religious organization for our lack
of spirituality does not help us with our view on God, nor
does it make us more spiritual.

I recall talking to a friend of mine who moved from
religion to religion, church to church, and different
spiritual organizations and yet still found the same
problems wherever he went. Not long after he would settle
in his "new spiritual place" in life he would find a problem
with the doctrine or the people. He kept trying to change
the outside circumstances without changing his internal
issues. He finally admitted to me that he was afraid of
being controlled. Yet the control didn't come from the
outside, it actually came from within: his old spiritual

belief system. Remember, no one can make you do anything. They can only influence you if YOU allow them. My friend had negative energy about his past spiritual experience and, just like a radio frequency he attracted more of that energy. The type energy you have about spirituality and God will either attract the right or wrong influence to you.

I am not saying that the religions of the world are not stained by man's own selfish desire, nor am I saying that we are blameless. Jim Rohn (author and motivational speaker) said, "For things to change we must change; for things to get better we must get better." Throwing out the baby with the bath water doesn't usually bring the results we are looking for. Just because we had a bad experience or no experience with religion or spirituality, doesn't mean we should stop pursuing spirituality or avoid it all together. In order to change our results we must go to the root of the problem.

We Attract What We Believe Most

If you are afraid of people taking advantage of you and this is your constant focus, then your mind will subconsciously find situations where people will take advantage of you. Your mind likes to fix problems so it will create a problem to be fixed. If this problem was not resolved in the past, the mind will recreate it so you have another chance to resolve it. There are however events that have happened to people, especially children, in which they were true victims without soliciting or inviting the abuse whether it is physically, emotionally, verbally or sexually. Being abused as a child has a domino effect that can be carried through adulthood. As an adult, the abused child's belief system regarding God, spirituality, and any other authority figure is distorted by the abuse.

Throughout this book, I speak briefly of the abuse that I have received from my father, but I was never specific of the type of abuse it was. A friend of mine who was helping me edit this book mentioned that I didn't really talk about what actually happened between me and my father. After she asked me a few probing questions, I realized that I was afraid of sharing the full story. I was afraid of what people would think of my dad. I was still protecting my father the same way I did when I was a kid. I remember my father telling me not to share with anyone what he was doing or he would get in trouble. My father has been dead for several years yet his words were still ringing in my head. As a result of this old belief, I became subconsciously selective of what and how much I would share in case I might hurt or damage his image. I decided, regardless of what anyone thinks, to not listen to the old tapes and to share with you what happened.

When I was growing up I was full of life and I was very trusting, especially with my father. He was my protector, provider and hero. It all came to a halt the night my father walked in my room and sexually abused me. It happened more than once. I was 5 years old. I remember being confused and feeling betrayed. I felt like I was worth nothing. I felt like an object to be used, abused then thrown away. My trust in any authority figure was shattered especially the ones who claimed to love me. My father was my hero who became the villain. He was the person who was supposed to protect me, but he ended up using the trust that I had for him to lure me into a trap. Guess what became my biggest struggle with God? Trust.

As I shared in the chapter on relationships, my "trust" file was programmed with "People who love you will lure you in and then pull the carpet out from under your feet". As an adult, I was introduced to the concept of God who claimed to love me and He wanted me to refer to Him as Father. He was supposed to be trustworthy. My mind had a very hard time differentiating between the physical father and my heavenly Father. I kept comparing God to my father. I subconsciously resisted trusting God. I was waiting for God to hurt me, always waiting for the other shoe to drop. As I shared in the chapter on relationships I was looking for evidence to not trust God. My mind needed to make the past right about the reason why I should not trust God.

As I shared, it was not just God but anyone who claimed they loved me, including my wife, friends at church, and pastors. I feared that someone would abuse or take advantage of me once again. I feared that I would be gullible as I was as a child when I trusted my father. I followed God at a distance for years and wondered why I could not fully trust him. I started to see patterns in my relationships. I kept attracting people with very dominant personalities who had deep issues and would take advantage of me. My boundaries were nonexistent because deep inside my heart I subconsciously believed that I deserved to be abused. My mind agreed and looked for relationships to fulfill what I believed.

As an adult, no one can control your choices, not even God. He gives us free will to follow him and trust him. He wants us to willingly follow him. We always have the freedom to choose. People have no power over us unless we allow them to influence our reaction when we hold on to the pain of our past. In other words, we can miss an amazing spiritual experience today because we are protecting ourselves from the pain of our past.

If we can take at least 1% of responsibility of our response or reaction to what happened to us in the past, then we can truly begin to take charge of our spirituality today. We must take responsibility for the belief system we've created. As I mentioned, I developed a very poor belief and image about God. I was actually subconsciously protecting myself from being abused by my father again, yet this time it wasn't my physical father but my spiritual Father.

Contradiction to What I Believed

Our foundation in life is our spirituality and our picture of God. These both can be different. You can believe in a concept of God and yet live a life contradictory to what you say you believe. As I shared, growing up my concept of God was distorted. However, my concept of my father (authority figure) was very clear since I was abused by him. On the other hand, I also believed that God must have been good since my mother had devoted so much of her life to Him. I had these two conflicting feelings about God based on my parents: God is good and He loves, but

He can't be trusted. As a result, I neglected my spirituality and avoided a relationship with God.

My soul was not being fed in a spiritual way. I didn't care to feed it spiritually. I just lived with a façade of a "happy" life hiding a starving soul. The emptiness of my soul was crying out for some kind of spiritual life, but I would feed it with women and material stuff. This vicious cycle only made the emptiness deeper.

Personal Spiritual Principles

When we create our own personal spiritual principle of life, we can easily break and justify our words. Since we call the shots for the standard of our spirituality, we can change on a whim to fit our lifestyle. I had my own spiritual standard which I kept breaking because my standard was based on whatever the crowd was doing or what I thought a moral life should be. For example, I would say, "I won't smoke weed anymore", but when an opportunity presented itself, I would justify my own standard by telling myself, "this is the last time". Well, "this is the last time" became every other day or whenever the occasion was right.

Why did I go back on my spiritual standards? I had no one to hold me accountable or help me live out my spiritual life. I just did whatever I felt was right in the moment. Based on my results, it wasn't working. As a matter of fact, I got to the point that I was seriously thinking about taking my own life. Life had lost all its meaning and purpose. My soul was not satisfied spiritually with the standard I came up with on my own.

If you say you have a spiritual standard for your life then write it down. Once you write it down, ask yourself how that standard you set is working for you. Another question to ask is did YOU really set your own standard or was it a belief system programmed from childhood. I used to argue that I didn't want to lose myself by being involved in any spiritual belief.

Yet the very thing I feared was happening without being involved in any spiritual activities. Your own spiritual standard may cause you to lose your true self. Your own standard without awareness of its true origin can cause you to be trapped in the prison of your own past spiritual belief system. This doesn't only happen to someone who sets their own spiritual standard of life, but also to the one who has a spiritual standard set for them in a religious setting. Either way the same result may follow: loss of self. Ask yourself who is actually setting your spiritual standard for life.

Most people follow spiritual leaders blindly and lose themselves in the process. Eventually, you will try to find what you have lost. If the leadership you are following becomes your God then you will eventually be hurt and walk away entirely from the concept of God or anything relating to Him. Because every human being is flawed and never meant to be put on a pedestal, they will guarantee to disappoint you. Look for God in God not in people.

Spiritual Emotional Charge

Have you ever felt so strongly about a cause and became so defensive that your reaction reflected the very opposite of what you stood for? I am not talking about passion, but your reaction or response to any opposition to your spiritual belief. Religious wars happen every day and they are mostly caused by what I call an emotional charge or a trigger. Religion is a very sensitive topic and it gets people pretty charged up in defending their point of view. Of course, since everybody thinks they have the right perspective, religious tension usually ends with a negative result. The real question we should be asking ourselves is where this emotional charge comes from.

As I said before we are charged up by past emotional experiences whether they were good or bad. Those experiences influenced our spiritual belief system. I believed I was already a Christian simply because my mother was a believer. I remember when I was young (not long before I became a Christian), my coworker asked me if I was a Christian. I got so upset at that question that I literally wanted to beat him up for even questioning my religion. The truth is I was not holding on to any kind of Christian belief and I had no clue what it meant to be a true Christian. I made up my own beliefs. So why was I so charged up? Questioning my faith caused a trigger to a memory of my mother's faith which was Christianity and because I loved my mother it felt like an attack on my mother. For some reason I felt connected with my mother's faith by our bond through family blood. I know I'm not the only one who believes in having faith through family blood. Did it have anything to do with Christianity? No, I never even read my bible once and no one ever explained Christianity to me. My emotional charge had nothing to do with religion but everything to do with an emotional memory of a spiritual belief system I created as a kid. My mother defined love for me and if anyone would threaten the picture I had of her I would get defensive.

What was picture was I trying to protect? I am glad you asked. The picture was the memory of my mom with God in perfect Harmony. It was the only picture that brought me some kind of peace. It was my own personal religion and it had nothing to do with her religion. I believe what fuels religious wars is the emotional charge from individuals who subconsciously connect with an experience of their past. In some countries, their history is stained by religious wars imprinted in the children of that country, some who grow up to become terrorists. Some people will say to me "I am so passionate about my spirituality or faith that I am compelled to react". If you search for the source of your reaction, you may be surprised to find that what you're fighting has everything to do with your mind being stuck in a belief system created from your past emotional memory.

Take some time to go back to your childhood and ask yourself with every positive or negative experience what spiritual belief system you created. How did the authority figures in your childhood influence your decisions about spiritual life today? There is a natural law of nature: we reap what we sow. If it's a seed of a fruit tree we will have a tree with that type of fruit. Fig trees grows figs, apple tree grows apples. So again, to see what kind of a "seed' we are planting we must take a look at the type of fruit we are producing. In other words the fruits are the results we produce in our lives regardless of what we claim to believe.

Fruits Reveals Who We Follow

As I mentioned before in the Emotional Awareness chapter, I was 5 years old when I created a "protector" or false self after I was abused. The protector was another side of me, a part of me who didn't want to allow anyone else to hurt me. He shut my emotions down and I decided not to trust anyone who would come close to my heart, which naturally produced fruits that were the opposite of love. As a result, I chose to become a Gangster when I was 16.

The more my protector ran my life, the more my life results or fruit reflected who I followed. The fruits were hate, anger, resentment, isolation, and ultimately self-destruction. These fruits showed up everywhere, especially in my relationships. Before I go on, I want to make something clear about the analogy of "protector" causing me to make bad decisions which produced these results. I am not saying or using "the devil made me do it" or "it's the protector's fault" as an excuse for the results in which I produce in my life.

Regardless, of who I created within me to trigger me to produce these results or fruits. I still had a choice. Victims believe that they only have one choice: to give in. They believe it's always somebody else's fault. Nothing in my life would have changed if I kept blaming someone else for my life's choices. I chose to listen to the wrong voices in my head. I chose to react emotionally. I chose to give in to what was comfortable. Until, at 21 years old, I took responsibility for my reactions, nothing changed. I took responsibility of the results I created in my life. I chose to replace my "Protector" with God. In other words, I redefined my definition of who God is and I started to listen to the right voices. My life was no longer based on my own standard but on God's standard.

I didn't accomplish this by myself; it took a spiritual community who were committed to teach me and help me walk the talk. I decided to follow God as my new authority figure in my life. As soon as God took the place as my true protector, the fruit or results in my life started to change. I became more patient, peaceful, loving, serving and forgiving to others. I am still far from being perfect and I still struggle with trusting people and even God. However, the overall fruits of my life are a night and day difference from who I was. The deep void in my heart that I talked about earlier was finally fulfilled.

"Fear of the Lord is the Foundation of Wisdom. Knowledge of the Holy one results in good judgment."~ Proverbs 9:10

The wrong knowledge I had of God, or anything spiritual, led me to make bad judgments in my life. To this day I still double check to see if I am still following a true belief of God. I base that judgment on the results that I produce in my life. I look to see if what I live matches what I believe. In the bible the fruits of the Spirits are described as love, peace, patience, kindness, goodness, faithfulness, gentleness, and self-control. These fruits, or lack of, are great indicators of where our heart is before God. They come from having roots in a spiritual foundation in God. The opposite of these fruits come from a guarded heart that has stopped loving. It doesn't mean He stopped loving us or He moved away from us. It can mean that we may love Him less and might have moved away from Him. It may also mean we are listening to the wrong voice and our roots are planted in the wrong foundation. When we judge ourselves by our own standards, we may either give ourselves too much credit or too little credit about how much we love God.

We have to hold ourselves accountable to a spiritual standard that's beyond our comfort zone and one that is not based on a human standard. I chose to hold myself to the bible's standard 18 years ago, and it has completely changed my life. I held myself accountable to my spiritual foundation by reading my bible daily, serving, praying and I also have people holding me accountable to that standard. Why would I go to all that trouble? I do this because it's easy to replace my current spiritual foundation (God's spiritual belief system) with the wrong foundation (anything other than God).

It's easy to get into a routine and drift away off course. It's easy to miss our own blind spots. I sometimes still subconsciously replace the true knowledge of God with the Knowledge of the Protector. The tendency that most of us have is to go back to what is familiar and comfortable. This is a great reason for you to have accountability for what you believe.

The Counterfeit Substitution of the True Foundation of Life

"When the storms of life come, the wicked are whirled away, but the godly have a lasting foundation" ~ *Proverbs 10:24 NLT*

A foundation is the most import structure of a building. Imagine for a minute, your life has a building made up of 4 walls. Picture the walls of this building representing our finances, our emotions, our relationships and our health. These walls are glued together and sustained by a foundation. If the foundation is shaky the whole building can fall apart. You may build a building (or life) that may look beautiful or even solid on the outside, but if it is not built on the right foundation, it will eventually fall apart. It may take years, but eventually it will happen. All it takes is the perfect storm. The perfect storm can come through a financial hit, an emotional disaster, conflict in our relationships, or through health issues. I believe a life built on God's foundation is the only true foundation that keeps this building called life in place. No matter what type of storms hit your building, it will still stand.

How would it really affect your life if you built a foundation using any of these four walls instead of a spiritual foundation? I was hoping you'd ask. Let's take a look at each of these walls and what each would look like built on the different foundations.

**A quick disclaimer before you read any further, our foundation can easily be replaced subconsciously by any of the other walls. If you realize you are building on a different

140

foundation other than a spiritual one, it doesn't mean all is lost. It means you subconsciously are building on the wrong foundation and all you need to do is to consciously start building on the right foundation. **

Health-Based Foundation

Let's start with health. If we put our hope solely on being healthy and/or on modern medicine to pull us through health challenges, we may find ourselves disappointed and hopeless. Especially if your health makes an unexpected turn for the worst and modern medicine can't come up with a solution. I will explain further on this point by sharing with you this amazing story;

A friend of mine was told by a very experienced doctor that her unborn child was going to have lung problems because of her health condition, and that she was about to deliver her baby prematurely. She had many problems throughout her pregnancy like throwing up blood and being rushed to the emergency room on many occasions. As a matter of fact, when she had her first baby she flat-lined during delivery. Her heart gave up and the doctors brought her back to life. Her experience with having a baby was already dramatic. To make matters worse, the same day and month two years before, when she died in the delivery room, was exactly on the same day and month of the delivery of this new baby. So you can imagine how afraid she must have been. She laid there on the same kind of hospital bed, looking at same kind of doctors talking to her before the delivery.

Her triggers must have been going off. However, this time she had something amazing going for her; a solid spiritual foundation in God and the support of a spiritual community praying for her. She prayed fervently and relied on faith, not her fears or what her doctors were predicting. She told me that she actually felt the prayers of her friends and it gave her peace. This is all part of her solid spiritual foundation which brought her amazing security. To the amazement of all the doctors, her baby was born 5 weeks early with healthy lungs. The doctors scratched their heads and could not believe it. It could have been worse, if she stressed out through the delivery. If all her faith was based on her health or what the doctors were telling her, she would have drowned in fear.

This is one of millions of stories out there about miracle healing or recovery. It is well documented that faith and spirituality (prayers) have caused many patients to be healed in a miraculous ways. Am I saying to do away with doctors and modern medicine? No way. We do need them. Yet relying solely on them, in my opinion, is a recipe for more stress in our lives. A Spiritual foundation must be laid first to withstand health challenges in our lives.

Our mind also needs to be healthy. A healthy mind is a positive mind. A spiritual mind is focused on spiritual things which are pure, noble, and praiseworthy. Again, a mind that is not anchored on a spiritual foundation can easily wander with self-destructive thoughts. Remember, most of our minds were programmed to think negative thoughts from childhood. Our thoughts must be captured and led into submission to match our spiritual standard.

The master of our thoughts should not be our mind; it should be the architect of our Spiritual Foundation: God.

As I shared in the chapter on Health, a person who has a positive thinking pattern will take care of their health. A man or woman truly rooted in a spiritual foundation will take care of their temple or body. He or she will understand that although they have the freedom to live healthy or unhealthy, they have an obligation to listen to the Healer within them: God. I am sure God wants you to be healthy. God, the Designer of your body, wants you to take care of his masterpiece.

Emotion-Based Foundation

"A feeling is a physical reaction to a thought"~Russell Friedman

A foundation based on emotions is intertwined with our thinking. Our thinking triggers our emotions. When you are at the end of your rope emotionally, where can you turn to? When you are stressed emotionally beyond what you can stand, what do you do? When your negative self-talks are hammering you and you're starting to believe what you are telling yourself, what do you do? As I said in the chapter on emotions, some people turn to either food, alcohol, drugs, sex, movies, books, or shopping, trying to fulfill something inside of them emotionally that can only be filled by spirituality or God. When we place our emotions as the foundation of life, then our emotions will be our master. What and how we feel will become our GPS in life.

Our emotions not anchored on a spiritual foundation will eventuality lead us to destroy ourselves or others. Emotions feed on other similar emotions. Fear feeds on insecurity, anger feeds on frustration and so on. The craving gets worse the more we feed these emotions, and eventually they take over our judgment. This is where addiction is born. Emotions can only take you so far. When logic disappears and you can't emotionally handle what is happening in your life, your emotions become a trap. Many have allowed their emotions to run them and end up losing everything in their lives.

For example, sexual lust is an emotion which can lead to many ruined relationships, and even to sexual abuse. It may be triggered by a wrong belief system of what it means to be loved or accepted. For some, being sexually desired equals being loved and accepted. As I shared before, my sexual abuse twisted my view of sexual desires. I subconsciously wanted to be desired sexually because it referred back to the abuse which was the first emotional encounter I had with being desired sexually. This triggered a yearning to be wanted in a lustful way. I subconsciously connected being loved and affectionate with being sexually desired or lusted after. Switching this way of thinking was like killing a part of me. I had to reprogram my mind to redefine what true love and acceptance meant through the eyes of my Creator instead of what my abuse taught me. Building on my new spiritual foundation gave birth to a new way of thinking about being sexually desired. The old belief system had to submit to the new belief system.

Sometimes we can confuse feeling spiritual and being spiritual. Just because you feel like you are spiritual does not mean you are. Emotions do not equal spirituality. When I feel good about God or my spiritual life, it does not necessarily mean I am doing well spiritually. My emotions have lied to me and led me astray spiritually many times. I am not saying to be a robot and disregard your passion or emotions about God or what you believe to be spiritual.

"Our feelings may be true indicators of what we are facing, but they don't need to dictate our decisions." ~ Lysa Terkhurst

Just because we feel passionate about something doesn't mean we are right. I am sure you have heard about terrorists killing others and themselves for a cause they believed to be spiritual. Passion was driven by their emotions. Being emotionally driven is not the same as being Spiritually Driven. Emotions are unstable and they can change every minute and every day, but a Spiritual foundation is solid because it is not based on how we feel. Being Spiritual is not supposed to be a one-time, "feel good", once a week on a Sunday deal. It's choosing to hold on to your spiritual standard even when you do not "feel" like it. For example, I would have never forgiven my father, if I based my forgiveness on how I felt. I would have quit following God as my authority figure as soon as someone from my church community hurt my feelings. I would not feel like waking up and spending quiet time with God because I would probably feel too tired.

The truth is, for most of us, we don't feel like doing the right thing because it feels like a part of us is dying. When we make a decision to change, we are choosing to kill the old belief system in order to allow the new belief system to live. You may experience depression, anger and resistance because you feel you are losing your old self. Our emotions and our thinking can lead us to a very dark place and cause us to live a life of shame and regret.

When your spiritual foundation is based on emotions you will see yourself going from one extreme to another. One moment you're the most loving person and helping the poor, and the next moment you are ready to kill the person cutting you off on the freeway. The fruits or results in your life will show you which foundation you are currently building your life on.

Relationship-Based Foundation

Our thinking and our emotions will determine the quality of relationships we build and who we surround ourselves with. Relationships are also an excellent way to gauge which foundation we are building on. An indicator of a relationship-based foundation is when you hold on to grudges and have a hard time forgiving people in your life. As I shared before in the chapter on emotions, the only person that gets the most pain is the person who holds on to the grudge. If you base your life's foundation on the status of your relationships, then your relationships will determine your spiritual commitment. What I mean is that if someone in your spiritual community hurts your feelings, then you may put up walls against that person or even walk away altogether. Yet we never stop to ask what does God want me to do? Is this decision in line with my spiritual beliefs? What does God think? Who is my best example on how to love?

God has unconditional love and when I am rooted in his love I have the strength to give that kind of love. Yet if I am rooted in a foundation based on emotions or based on human relationships, I will limit my ability to love. When your heart is centered on God's foundation you will fight a lot more to bring unity versus disunity in your relationship. I don't mean that if you have a dysfunctional relationship where you are being abused or in danger to stick to it. This may be a red flag for you to rebuild your relationship on a foundation based on God. In some cases, you may have to remove yourself from the relationship in order to rebuild yourself spiritually. However, each person will need to take personal responsibility for building their own spiritual foundation in order to bring true peace and unity.

If your foundation is based on spirituality, you will have to keep on pushing yourself to love more and not think you have "arrived". You will have to give up your rights to be right, and swallow your pride. That kind of love requires you to be open-minded and humble to how to love. An open-minded person will jump on the opportunity to learn how to increase their love for other people. On the other hand, when you feel your standard of love is already great then you subconsciously (or consciously) stop learning how to love. When you are not growing you're dying. A hungry man will work for food, but a man with a full stomach will barely lift his finger to work. The burning desire to improve happens only when you realize that you are lacking something. Another indicator of a dying love is when you become defensive when someone questions the measure of your love for others. Then you start blaming and justifying your reaction because of how someone else reacted. You may say to yourself, "I will change when they change". This is a very conditional way of loving.

As I have seen and consulted many couples who have subconsciously built their relationships based on human standards, and they eventually turn on each other. The fruits of these relationships eventually produce bitterness, hatred, and revenge. Any relationship based on anything other than a spiritual foundation is only a skeleton of what that relationship could be. I am not saying if you're not spiritual you cannot have a functional relationship. I am saying you will never know about a true fulfilling relationship in a spiritual way because it cannot be accomplished by human effort alone. Think about that. If there was a way to improve or increase the love in your relationships in a supernatural way, why wouldn't you want that? If it could be better, why not try it and see how your relationship changes?

In your defense you may be saying that you have seen many believers, or people who claim to be spiritual, that had horrific relationships. That's very true. However, just because someone claims to have a spiritual foundation, doesn't mean they are living what they preach. Remember, most of us run our lives subconsciously, meaning we are not fully aware of what we do. Just because you labeled yourself a Christian or a spiritual person doesn't mean you are automatically living out what you say you believe. Always start by looking for the results in your relationships and it may lead you to the cracks in your own foundation. You have two choices; you can ignore them or change the whole foundation.

Before I switched my foundation from my own standard to God's standard for my relationships, I had a track record of failed relationships. My relationships became my god or master. I would pour myself into relationships only to feel empty. I would put a heavy burden and pressure on my relationships because I relied fully on them to be my savior. I wanted them to save me from the void I felt inside. I kept being let down and disappointed. Nevertheless, I became co-dependent in my relationships. I started to compare what I produced my relationships to my friends who switched to a spiritual foundation. Their relationships and their fruit were way better looking than mine. I couldn't argue with God's track record.

I realized that my best effort and thinking didn't get me too far, so I surrendered and tried God's way. Once I did that, I dated an amazing, spiritual, beautiful woman who I have been happily married to for 13 years. Now that's a miracle, not only about the quality of the person I met, but the fact that I have been faithful to one person this long. This was an impossible task when I relied on my own standard. Knowing my own relationship track record, I know for a fact that what keeps my marriage together is my relationship rooted in God's foundation. To this day, the minute I switch foundations, is the minute my relationship suffers. It doesn't mean it's always heaven on earth, but the times I get angry, disrespectful, blaming, and demand my own way, I know I am disconnected with my spiritual foundation.

Financial-Based Foundation

Our finances without a healthy spiritual foundation can get us in major trouble. We have all seen numbers of major corporations corrupted with greed as they took advantage of many families' retirement accounts. A foundation that is based only on making money and being financially successful can easily become our master. Greed creeps in very easily when finances become the foundation of our lives. It can destroy your relationships as it did for my friend who focused all his attention on his success and ended up losing his marriage in the process.

When I made six figures in 45 days, I thought that it was going to fulfill me, but it just left me feeling empty. I realized later that my foundation had become about my finances and success. I was so focused on making more money and being successful that I attached my self-worth to my success. When I lost my properties and my income in the real state crash, my self-worth was crushed. I didn't feel like a man. I felt unworthy. I felt that I would be better dead than alive. (You can read more about my story in the chapter on finances). When your self-worth is defined by what you have in the bank or your success, this may be an indicator that your foundation is built on finances alone. When your self-worth is defined by God's spiritual principles, even if your success or bank account goes to negative zero you can still have a healthy self-worth. Why? God's foundation is based on love which has nothing to go with what material or financial success you have.

When we build our finances on a spiritual foundation, we naturally start shifting to generous heart. Just about every book written on finances says something about tithing or being generous and being ethical financially as the best ways to accumulate wealth. These are all based on spiritual principles rooted from a spiritual foundation.

"You reap what you sow" or "it's a numbers game" are phrases I used to hate hearing because it meant I had to put in the work in order to get what I wanted and things didn't just come to me. For the longest time, I wanted to give the least while expecting to gain the most in return. Yet when I applied spiritual principles on my finances, giving became more satisfying than receiving.

When you replace God as your life's foundation, it will affect where and what you invest in financially. For example, if your foundation is based on emotions your financial decisions will be driven by your emotions, like fear or greed. Your investing and spending will be controlled by your emotions. Some people commit suicide when all their finances are gone.

If your financial foundation is built on relationships, you may become a financial rescuer helping people by saving them every time they are drowning financially. You may eventually find them in the same financial mess down the line and the process will repeat itself. You will soon realize that you are really enabling people to remain financially irresponsible instead of empowering them to take responsibility for their own finances. You will become an ATM for your friends and family. You will eventually become bitter and become a victim yourself. Then you will lash out at them for taking advantage of you.

Of course, not all cases are the same but I think you know what I am talking about. When you build your finances on a spiritual foundation, your finances becomes a source of help for many people and you become an extension of God's love through your finances. It does not mean you give everything away. It means your giving is focused and your money goes further with spirit-driven force rather than human-driven force. You are empowering people through your finances while not taking the place of a savior or rescuer. As you can see, any foundation we build our lives on other than a spiritual foundation will crash when the storms of life hit. Life has too many storms to build it on any other foundation.

Learning Retention rate

"Knowledge without application is useless, but knowledge with application is powerful" ~ Mikki Wade

Now that we have clarified which foundation to build on, let's look at the reasons why so many people don't live what they preach or what they claim their foundation is. I found it very interesting to see how much we really retain of what we learn. Here is some research done on learning retention rate:

> "Original research done by Edgar Dale on the effectiveness of learning or the learning retention rate based on the learning experiences and the media that was used for the instruction, is shown in the

following table. From Dale's research, additional studies were performed by the National Training Laboratory Institute for Applied Behavioral Science and many others." (Table below)

adapted from *http://www.tenouk.com/learningretentionrate.html*

Teaching Method	Knowledge Retention
See/Hear - Lecture	5%
Reading	10%
Audio Visual / Video	20%
Demonstration	30%
Discussion Group	50%
Practice by Doing	75%
Teaching Others	90%
Immediate application of learning in a real situation	90%

Did you read that? We retain only 5% of what we hear and see and 10% of what we read. This means, If you go to church or a spiritual gathering once a week to hear a message (which helps you to build your spiritual foundation), you only retain 5%. That's not much spiritual building material to keep you from slipping back into subconsciously building your life on a different foundation.

You may be going to spiritual gatherings and/or reading spiritual books regularly. Good for you. That takes you to 10% or maybe even 20% retention rate. If you are only retaining 20% in those activities, then what does your mind do with rest of the time? You must be retaining something else: your old belief system; whatever your mind retains from the media or what is socially accepted; whatever new spiritual trend you hear; or what your parents or grandparents might be advising. Your mind is always learning something. No wonder we can switch foundations so fast without even realizing it. If you rely solely on going to church or a spiritual gathering hearing and reading the message once a week, you may still be spiritually starving.

Again, those activities are important and very good building material for your spiritual foundation, but they are just not enough. Your retention rate for what you learn is directly impacted by whatever foundation you claim to have or believe in. In other words, you still have to do the work to retain or you will forget what you've learned. I've found that most people don't fully invest in learning more about their life's foundation. They just go with the flow with whatever the day might bring. If you are only reading and listening you are not retaining much and you will most likely switch foundations.

Take another look at the chart above; you retain 75% from practicing by doing what you believe or learn. Just like riding a bike, building a solid spiritual foundation will take a lot of practice by doing. All the thinking in the world about riding will not teach you how to ride a bike, you actually have to ride it. In the same way, you can just think about doing something spiritual or building a spiritual foundation without taking action. A 75% retention rate from practicing by doing is a major jump from the 20% retention rate from listening and hearing. I don't know about you, but I like to retain as much as I can, especially if the quality of my spiritual life depends on it. I take that pretty seriously and I know you do too.

Let's take another look at the chart. You retain 90% by teaching others and/or immediately applying what you learn in a real situation. But, what real situation are we talking about here? Any real situation that you would face in your life, would be good or bad situations in your relationships, situations you're dealing with emotionally, situations in your Health or in your finances. In other words, any situation you come across in your life.

How about teaching others? I believe that is another great way to retain because it holds you accountable. The best advice you give is the one you need to listen the most. However, I believe you need to first apply the knowledge of your spiritual foundation to your own life before you can start to teach others. The blind should not lead the blind. There is no way you can just cruise through life without double checking your spiritual foundation. You can't leave it to chance; you have to be applying what you believe.

This scripture brings this point home, "*22 Do not merely listen to the word, and so deceive yourselves. Do what it says. 23 Anyone who listens to the word but does not do what it says is like someone who looks at his face in a mirror 24 and, after looking at himself, goes away and immediately forgets what he looks like. 25 But whoever looks*

155

intently into the perfect law that gives freedom, and continues in it – not forgetting what they have heard, but doing it – they will be blessed in what they do." James 1:22-23

This was written thousands of years ago, before Edgar Dale did his research. This spiritual truth is still proven to be true to this day. Whatever foundation you claim to have, you still should double check it and follow through with what you claim to believe. If you don't, you will forget what you look like, your own reflection or the accurate truth about you, and which foundation you are building on. You may be thinking to yourself, I can't do this on my own. You may have tried and fell short. The truth is that you and I were never supposed to do this all by ourselves. We all need support through a spiritual support system or spiritual community. Before you shut me out and tell me how you've been hurt by relying on a spiritual community or organized religion, let's take a closer look at what I mean by a spiritual support system or community.

Spiritual Support System or Community

The majority of people I have met have been hurt by a support system or by people in an organized religion. As I mentioned before, the words "organized religion" can trigger people to become angry based on the hurt that was caused in the name of religion. The hurt may have come from abuse by a spiritual leader, being harshly judged by a spiritual group, being forced to go to church by an authority figure, or an experience of division within a spiritual group. As a result, some people don't want anything to do with God or any spiritual community. Let me be straightforward with you, any group which involves people will have dysfunction in it.

By now, I hope you know that I acknowledge and validate your pain and am in no way dismissing what happened to you or what you feel. On the other hand, I also have met some people who act like the hurt from similar experiences never happened to them. They end up hiding behind a spiritual act. They are busy serving in the name of their belief, but their heart is far away from a real connection to God and others. They keep themselves busy serving so no one will suspect that they need help. No one can hide their pain forever, because it will be projected on others no matter how much you try to hide. I believe many of these people are repeating a cycle, which was probably similar to the cycle of whoever hurt them. Throughout this book I write about the belief system overriding whatever you claim to say or feel. Your past repeats itself when you do not deal with your pain. You may have a sincere heart about your spirituality, but your fruits will show you the truth about your beliefs.

We need other people to keep us on track with our spiritual foundation. Your life will crumble all around you without a healthy spiritual foundation just as much as it will crumble without a strong spiritual support system. You need both.

There was an interesting study done over a 4-week period on support systems and goals that pertains to the point I am trying to make. Participants of this study were randomly assigned to one of 5 condition groups:

Group 1- Unwritten Goal

Group 2- Written Goal

Group 3- Written Goal & Action Commitments

Group 4- Written Goal, Action Commitments to a Friend

Group 5- Written Goal, Action Commitments & Progress Reports to a Friend

At the end of the 4 weeks participants were asked to rate their progress and the degree to which they had accomplished their goals. According to the study, the 5th group had the most productive results, because they had an accountability partner. Someone else had to hold them accountable to their own commitments. If your goal is truly to build a solid spiritual foundation, then you need to be committed to a community that will support you. Within that community you need a partner(s); someone or a few people who have similar beliefs. This group can help you see your blind spots. They can help redirect you back to your spiritual foundation.

Finding a Good Support System

In the Relationship Awareness chapter, I talked about focusing on healing your inner world so your outer world will be healed. Since you take yourself wherever you go, you need to become more concerned about first changing your own spiritual foundation. In other words, your spiritual support system starts with you. It starts with you becoming the example of the person you want others to be for you. If you want others to be loyal and committed, then you become a loyal and committed friend first. Walking away when things gets rough, without doing the best that you can in finding a solution, is not an example of a loyal and committed friend.

We need to become solution-oriented versus problem-oriented. If you bring up a problem, you better have a solution attached to it. It doesn't take much effort or courage to point out what's wrong with something or some group without doing anything about it. So to be clear, I don't mean you have to stay in a place where you're getting abused. Look for your own past pattern, and see what you can do differently before running away. Remember, wherever you go there will be people, and it's inevitable for people to hurt and disappoint you.

Recently, I was teaching this concept to a friend who wanted to be involved in my church community. I guaranteed him one thing; people in this community will hurt and disappoint him. I told him this may not be done purposely, but it's inevitable, because we are human and not gods. I wanted my friend to build his foundation on God instead of relationships. If you have a hard time being committed with your current group now, I guarantee you will have a hard time committing to the one you will replace it with.

I had another friend, who asked me if he could be part of my small group. He said he had a hard time reconnecting his heart spiritually. He also had issues with the way things ran in our church. I challenged him to come to my group with the focus on giving not just taking. I told him that I would support him, but if he came "expecting" or feeling entitled to be supported he would be disappointed. I knew my friend had a lot to give, but I also knew he held back because of the pain he had from his experience in our church. In time, my friend's attitude started to change and he began to give his heart to my group. His impact brought the rest of the people in the group closer. He started to give more than what he received. By doing this, he was changing.

One day, I asked my group if there was anything they wanted me to pray about. My friend asked me to pray for his heart. He wanted to be less critical of his spiritual community. Even though he loved my small group and was fully engaged in it, he had a new desire to be re-engaged in the bigger spiritual community or church. He wanted to give the same way he did when he first got involved in our church. When he first came to our church, he had young innocent heart without blemish, but after being hurt a few times, his heart began to close up. Over the years, he distanced his heart from fully giving to this community. Now, he wanted prayers for his heart to expand the capacity of his love for his spiritual community again.

Several months later, he went to the hospital because he was not feeling well. The doctors couldn't figure out what was wrong with him. He was not doing well. He could barely breathe the first day I saw him at the hospital. I will never forget what he said the 4th day of being in the hospital. You see, his first week in the hospital was filled with friends from his spiritual community visiting him.

They came in by the truck load. He told me that he gets it. He sees what the community is about. He told me, he couldn't understand how much he was loved by this community until he didn't have the strength to give anything back, but only receive their love. He heard about their love when someone in the community was in need, but never really experienced it. However, this circumstance forced him to experience their love for him. He saw God's love in action through this community.

This community loved him unconditionally; the very community that he was wary about giving his full heart to. It was obvious that this community had their foundation based on God, and not just on other relationships. As he shared his gratitude with tears and laughter, I stood in awe. The prayer he requested for his heart was answered before my eyes. He told me he didn't want to forget this experience and couldn't wait to get out of the hospital to be fully engaged with his community. Unfortunately, my friend never made it out of the hospital. He died 3 weeks later.

I remember the last week of his life there was over 30 people coming in and out of that hospital. I heard one of the nurses that took care of him ask if he was famous. Another nurse answered; no he is just a man who is loved. "A man who is loved". That's what I want my community to be known for: their love for each other.

At his funeral over a hundred people showed up. He gave more than he realized. His spiritual community loved him unconditionally and grieved for him as a mother would grieve for her child. He had truly built his life's foundation on a spiritual solid foundation and community rooted in God.

The point of my story is that you will not find a perfect community, but you can heal your heart and it will open your eyes to see that what you need is not perfection but gratitude. When you focus on healing your heart, the right community will show up. When you focus on being the solution, you will see more of the solution than the problem.

You may already be in the right community, I don't know. What I do know is that you will not be able to see it if you are clouded by resentment, criticalness, and ingratitude. You will be so blinded by your own wounds that you won't be able to see the healing you need already around you. Remember, the belief system you use to build your spiritual foundation will direct where you go and which community you will be drawn to.

Choosing the Right Support System

"When the student is ready the teacher will appear."
Buddhist Proverb

When you start living out what you believe, the match with your spiritual community will be organic. You will come in and feel at home. You will know because you will see your values lived out.

Earlier I shared about the amazing love the community had for my friend. It is one of the most important qualities of any spiritual community. A healthy spiritual community should be defined by their love for God and for others. Love should be clearly evident in that community. If you show up to this community and no one cares if you are there or not, or you don't see people loving God and each other, then you may have a problem. If you are experiencing this (or have in the past) it can only be one of two things; either you are not engaging your heart or you need to look for another community that fits your spiritual values. That being said, I believe the first place to look for change is in your heart before you change your surroundings or community. Not the other way around.

I spoke briefly about a small group within a bigger community. It's such an important part of your support system that I am going spend a little more time on that topic. You need to belong to a small group of people within a big community. It's easy to be lost in a group of 50 or 100 plus people, because it's hard to be open and real with a lot of people at one time. We need a group that is really involved in each other's life. A group that will hold us accountable and support us to live out what we profess. I have been involved in different small groups and I can tell you that not all groups are created equal.

In the past 17 years I have been involved in small groups in my church and have never experienced a group that didn't lack something. However, the thing that kept me faithful to this imperfect community for all these years was some great advice given to me by the first person who introduced me to my spiritual foundation and spiritual community. He told me that regardless of what other people do, I need to hold on to my spiritual values because

I am personally responsible to build my own spiritual foundation.

His advice came from a scripture quoting a line from Jesus, "If you hold to my teaching, you are really my disciples. Then you will know the truth and the truth will set you free." (John 8:31-32) It doesn't say if someone else is not holding to God's teaching, then it's okay to let go and use that has an excuse to leave and do whatever I want.

To drive the point home, my friend told me that even if he personally stopped holding on to this spiritual foundation, I should not walk away. Ironically, many years later, he walked away from his spiritual foundation and his community. I was crushed, disappointed, and in disbelief. It was a tough storm. Even though it rocked me emotionally, it didn't rock my foundation, because it wasn't built on that relationship. It is built on a spiritual relationship with God.

Conclusion
The Architect of You

I recently saw the TV series *Prison Break*. It was about an innocent person being condemned to death for a crime he didn't commit. He had a brother who was an architect and was completely devoted to getting his brother out of prison. One day, the architect brother (who also happened to be the one who designed the prison's blueprint) purposely robbed a bank and made sure he got caught so he would be sent to the same prison as his brother. He knew all the ways out of that prison and had a very thorough plan to get his brother out.

God has a thorough plan to free you from the prison of your mind and emotions. He wants you to have freedom from your "protector" and your negative, unhealthy belief systems. You have been trapped in this prison for too long and have been held back from living out your dreams. This freedom can only be found in a solid foundation in God, and this foundation will build a life that you thought was impossible. I shared with you the emptiness, the brokenness in my relationships, and that my life was without meaning. Now what I thought was impossible has become possible as I look at my life and my relationships. I never imagined that I could find my true self and live a full life as a "dreamer".

Our physical and emotional image of our fathers can distort the image of our Heavenly Father. Even if you had no physical father, there are still belief systems running you (from having a fatherless childhood) which directly impacts your view of God. You may have had a dad who was too busy to spend time with you or was not emotionally available. You may have had a mother who was not there for you when you needed her the most to comfort you through painful trials. Maybe you yearned for a loving touch or to hear the words "I love you" and got the opposite. Or maybe, like me, who you thought was supposed to be your hero and protector became your predator. You were left in prison. Whatever you've experienced was in the past. God wants to free you from being trapped by your past and your fear of the future. He has already secured the right community for you. He wants to give you a brand new F.R.E.S.H. (Finances, Relationships, Emotions, Spiritual, and Health ™) start.

This is your life, your choice. I once heard someone say that life is a temporary assignment. You can mechanically run through this assignment with what you are currently doing and continue getting the same results, or you can allow a supernatural being to change you from the inside out. Attempting to change on your own without His help will only lead you back to your self-made prison. It takes the Architect who designed your life and knows everything about you to change you. God designed you for something more than just surviving in this world. He designed your life for a purpose. Let HIM be the GPS of your life. No matter how frustrating life gets, remember…

You are not alone.

ABOUT THE AUTHOR

Mikki Wade is the founder and CEO of True Reality, Inc., an inspirational speaker, life coach and author. Born in Central Africa, Mikki's childhood was not an easy one. Like many, his family was a dysfunctional one and as a result he didn't have a good relationship with his father. His mother, however, meant the world to him. When Mikki was 12, his father moved him and his siblings back to America where he was originally from. Mikki's mother, however, stayed behind. She died the following year and, living miles away, Mikki never got to say goodbye.

With his mother gone, Mikki became involved in street gangs. But at the age of 18 he decided this was not the life for him. A few years later Mikki accepted an invitation to church which began the road to discovery and learning how to have a balanced life in spite of his circumstances.

Also ambitious, Mikki fostered his entrepreneurial spirit and started his own business at 27. By the time Mikki was 34, he was making an impressive sum of money selling home loans. At one point, he made $110,000 in 45 days. Mikki finally felt successful. Then he attended a life changing seminar which altered his view of success. He realized that working hard and spending harder wasn't any way to live. He was defining success by someone else's standard.

Today, Mikki measures his success by balance; balanced Finances, Relationships, Emotions, Spirituality and Health (F.R.E.S.H.). Mikki desires to share how others can be balanced too through his workshops and his dream to start a school called the F.R.E.S.H. Hope Academy that teaches young children about these five key areas.

For More Information

You can go to www.truerealityinc.com to find out more information about the workshops and visit www.freshhopeacademy.org to find out more about how you can support his dream of teaching our children these important and vital life skills.

Made in the USA
Columbia, SC
26 December 2022

74976591R00109